American Pilgrimage

American Pilgrimage

Sacred Journeys and Spiritual Destinations

Mark Ogilbee and Jana Riess

PARACLETE PRESS
BREWSTER, MASSACHUSETTS

2006   First Printing

Copyright © 2006 by Mark Ogilbee and Jana Riess

ISBN 1-55725-447-8

Library of Congress Cataloging-in-Publication Data
Ogilbee, Mark.
   American pilgrimage / by Mark Ogilbee and Jana Riess.
      p. cm.
   ISBN 1-55725-447-8 (alk. paper)
   1. Sacred space—United States. 2. Pilgrims and pilgrimages—
United States. 3. United States—Religion. 4. Spiritual life. I. Riess,
Jana. II. Title.
   BL2525.035 2006
   203'.50973—dc22   2006002755

10 9 8 7 6 5 4 3 2 1

Published by Paraclete Press
Brewster, Massachusetts
www.paracletepress.com
Printed in the United States of America.

For my wife, Caroline Lee, who never stops believing.

—MO

For my husband, Phil Smith, whose love
makes all things possible.

—JR

CONTENTS

J ust inside the entrance to the Abbey of Gethsemani in Kentucky is a new building, a pristine visitors' center added in 2004 to meet the needs of the growing number of people who want to pop in there: old and young, from many religious traditions and all walks of life. As the monastery's reputation has grown—it is the oldest and the largest Trappist monastery in the United States—it's no longer just retreatants who want to visit. Gethsemani has become something of a tourist attraction.

The visitors' center highlights the important distinction between a tourist and a pilgrim: The tourist is all about the destination and what can be obtained there. Such visitors file off the buses at Gethsemani, part of excursions that may also stop at a bourbon distillery or Churchill Downs. They enjoy an informative film about the monastery, and may have a brief opportunity to interact with a monk. They make their purchases of postcards, fudge, and cheese. And then they go home, satisfied that they have sampled the basic flavor of the place and can paste some photos of it in their scrapbooks.

A pilgrim is after another experience entirely. For the pilgrim, Gethsemani is not a means to an end so much as a journey in and of itself. If the tourist is a consumer, venturing forth to acquire something tangible to prove she has been there, then the pilgrim is more like a participant observer, pausing on the path to take stock of where she has been and where she is going.

This is a book for pilgrims. It's about going deeper, and journeying to places—both external and internal—that we might not expect. At Gethsemani, for example, the "real" action happens farther in and further down, past the visitors' center by the road: It happens in the guest house, where people's lives are changed by retreating from the world for a time; it happens in the church, where the monks cycle through chanting the Psalms every two weeks; it happens in the cloister, where the fortress-like walls ironically promise spiritual freedom. Casual tourists glimpse the place but don't necessarily *see* it; pilgrims connect with

Gethsemani and other sacred sites on a wholly different level.

What makes a trip a pilgrimage? Pilgrimage is about stepping back, reflecting, and spending time in greater spiritual awareness. In this book, our model for the pilgrimage journey is "transition before transformation." When we become pilgrims, we become boundary-crossers, slipping out beyond our normal borders and limitations to other, more spiritual, realms. In most pilgrimages, we undertake a physical journey to a place apart, though few modern pilgrims—in America at least—walk hundreds of miles to get there, as did the saints of old.

Sometimes, the borders we must cross involve not just space but time, as when we sacrifice a precious week of vacation to reflect on our lives at a monastery such as Gethsemani or the Community of Jesus. To understand this, it's useful to think about time the way the ancient Greeks did. They had two separate but complementary concepts of time: *chronos* and *kairos*. Chronos was the everyday, by-the-sundial time that ordinary people used to organize their meals, sporting events, and workdays. Kairos time was a different kettle of fish. These same ordinary people saw kairos as time out of time. It was not quotidian but special— a time for heightened awareness and understanding. For many people today, a pilgrimage offers the chance for kairos time, for hours and days stolen from the demands of the ticking chronos metronome.

Moreover, boundary-crossing is about transcending the limitations we've put on God and the ways the divine is at work in our lives. Pilgrimage explodes our notions about who, and, perhaps more important, where, God is. Pilgrimage tells us that God is everywhere—witness the appearances of Mary in such profane and unexpectedly domestic places as a piece of breakfast toast or a sheet hanging on the line. But many of us find God to be most accessible in sites worn smooth by the footprints of all the pilgrims who came before us. A woman named Denise ventured to India, for example, to take advantage of more advanced yoga instruction and the deepened spiritual awareness she expected to find there. It turned out to be a terrible and rather dangerous trip, however, and the enlightenment she sought proved elusive. Returning home, she realized an important truth. "I think after the whole ordeal I realized that I had never felt more in tune with my spirituality than when I was in smoggy, congested, and materialistic L.A., than the 'holy' land of India," she wrote later. "But I guess I would never have believed this if I hadn't gone on this journey myself." Pilgrimage for Denise helped her recognize that divine encounters can occur almost anywhere if we remain open to them. Ironically, she had to go to India to come to this realization. Like Denise, when we make this deep inner transition into pilgrimage, opening ourselves for change, we might experience the long-hoped-for transformation. It comes, however, from beyond, outside our control. That is the gift of pilgrimage.

Pilgrimages don't have to be far-off ordeals—what Chaucer called "distant shrines renowned in sundry lands"—to be special. The word "pilgrimage" may conjure up a lone backpacker taking an entire summer off to hike the trail of Santiago de Compostela through France and Spain, and those extended journeys are certainly wonderful. Your co-authors, who are longtime friends with an interest in travel, have separately enjoyed wide-ranging travel experiences in Europe, India, Israel, Egypt, and Central America, and we cherish those memories of discovery. But part of the reason we wanted to write this book is to communicate that people don't have to venture to exotic lands to go on pilgrimage. Readers who don't have the time or money to travel to Medjugorje or Benares or Lourdes—or whose health is too precarious to endure such a journey—will find that many remarkable places are available right in our own backyards. The places discussed in this book have wonderful histories, and powerful stories of people's deepening connections with God. We've intentionally selected sites that are scattered in different regions of the country, so most readers will have at least a few within driving distance.

We also believe that there can be something uniquely American about pilgrimage—that Americans can put their particular stamp on pilgrimage and add something new to age-old experiences. For starters, one of the most unusual and rather wondrous aspects of American religion is its flexibility and porousness. Pilgrimage, as we've said, is all about crossing boundaries, both literal and figurative, and one of the most significant boundaries to surmount is our human tendency to categorize God in terms of human institutions and denominations. In this book we'll see non-Catholics who pray to St. Jude or chant the divine office at Gethsemani; Christians who follow the teachings of Buddhist leader Thich Nhat Hanh or sample the spiritual waters of the New Age hot spot Sedona, Arizona; and people from all traditions who feel compelled to make the walk to Chimayó on Good Friday. All of these are examples of a kind of boundary crossing; we expand the comfortable confines of the tradition we know to try to access the sacred in a fresh way.

In America, also, we have what could politely be called a shallow history, so Americans have made pilgrimage sites out of some unlikely places. At the Healing Rooms in California's Santa Maria Valley, the site itself is underwhelming; it's housed mostly in the Sunday school classrooms of an ordinary, modern American church. What makes it a powerful pilgrimage site is the resolute expectation of the faithful, who come here from all over the world to pray for a miracle. The Healing Rooms underscore an important aspect of pilgrimage in general and American pilgrimage in particular: creativity. People bring *to* the site what they need *from* the site.

Some pilgrimages are about the power of place—even secular pilgrimages, such as to memorials and battlefields. We marvel at Gettysburg, for example, enthralled that the most terrible battle of American history took place on the very soil where we are standing. We go to these places to remember specific events, and fuse the past and the present together in an unbroken chain of meaning. In this book, several of the sacred sites we explore are likewise very much about the pull of a particular locale. Graceland, for instance, is significant not because of its much-maligned décor, but because it was Elvis's longtime home; it is a modern relic of a secular saint, and people invest it with profound religious meaning. And in Chimayó, New Mexico, the very earth is resonant; pilgrims believe that Chimayó's famous healing properties are found quite literally in the dirt itself, so any pilgrimage to Chimayó is by necessity an actual physical journey.

But sometimes it's not necessary to travel to a particular place to experience the authentic spiritual riches it has to offer. Although many people do make the trip to the

National Shrine of Saint Jude in Chicago when they have an especially desperate reason to seek the intervention of the patron saint of hopeless causes, far more pray to Jude in their homes or neighborhood parishes, engaging in an inward pilgrimage that is every bit as meaningful to them as a voyage to his shrine.

In English, we have just one basic word to describe all of these kinds of experiences, whereas other languages have distinctive terms for different forms of pilgrimage, like a ritual for a national holy day versus a visit to a local shrine. But the truth is that every pilgrimage is unique. Sometimes we go on pilgrimage with a very clear idea of what we're seeking, like the people praying for healing at the Healing Rooms in Santa Maria, California. At other times we stand at the threshold of a pilgrimage experience without a clearly defined idea of what we need or desire. Some places, such as the Abbey of Gethsemani, require a degree of introspection and retreat from the world, while other experiences, such as attending a Billy Graham crusade, are inherently communal and social. Some pilgrimages are rooted in a particular faith tradition and appeal primarily to people of that tradition; other sites are permeable to outsiders, or stand on the outside of tradition themselves.

In every case, however, pilgrimage is always a journey of transformation, a voyage of the heart. What unites the various kinds of pilgrimage explored in this book is that we did not depart from these places as quite the same people we were when we entered them. The pilgrim, by definition, makes progress; we must move forward. As T.S. Eliot once wrote, "we must be still and still moving into another intensity." Pilgrimage is about opening ourselves to change and growth, and inviting new experiences to alter our perspective.

Every place we visited in the research for this book taught us something different about ourselves and the pilgrimage experience. At the Community of Jesus, co-author Jana Riess learned a valuable lesson about the liberating power of honesty. The following story illustrates what this entire book seeks to communicate: People come to sacred spaces hoping to be changed.

I arrived for my retreat a day late and *sans* luggage, which had not made it to Cape Cod; the suitcase would begrudgingly appear shortly before my departure. In the absence of my clothes, books, and cosmetics, I put the limits of the famed Benedictine hospitality to the test. In the sixth century, Saint Benedict had stipulated that every guest be received as Christ himself, and I think he would be delighted with the way the sisters cared for me and quietly outfitted me with the essentials. While it was disappointing not to have my own things, I felt God's love through the sisters' attention to detail.

But more than that, not having my objects of comfort opened me up for a profound spiritual experience. Sitting in the back of the Church of the Transfiguration at Saturday vespers, my heart stirred as the Community's internationally renowned choir sang the benediction from the narthex just behind me. As I felt their blessing wash over me and the sopranos hit a piercing crescendo, tears began trickling down my face. These tears I hastened to wipe away: *Someone might see; my mascara will smudge; I'm here as a professional writer, for heaven's sake!* And then I was hit by the force of what people had been trying to tell me in interview after interview all during my time at the Community: What distinguishes it as a holy place is the fact that we can be our real selves there, without the masks that we feel we need to wear all of the time. I let the tears flow, no longer concerned about my mascara. Because by some remarkable confluence of divine providence and airline incompetence, my cosmetics bag had never arrived, and I remembered I was wearing no makeup to speak of. With this realization came a second: It wasn't just a facial mask I was lacking, but a spiritual one; my most raw, ugly, and unguarded self had shown up for worship, and that unholy person was being blessed by the choir. I wept for the sheer joy of the reprieve.

Such experiences are the gift of pilgrimage. In the end, pilgrimage is about discovery, both spiritual and personal. While the sites we gravitate toward may be different, and our chosen experiences will vary greatly, the core objective of all pilgrimage experience is always transformation. It is our hope that this book and some of the sites we include here will become for you vehicles of spiritual renewal and change, bringing you closer to God. To that end, we include one appendix with suggestions for further reading and another with additional information about the various places we discuss in the book. We also hope that you are able to take whatever deeper perspective you acquire on pilgrimage and apply it to all your travel experiences. As Phil Cousineau put it in *The Art of Pilgrimage,* "How might we use that wisdom to see more soulfully, listen more attentively, and imagine more keenly on *all* our journeys?"

PART ONE

Pilgrimages of Healing

People have long associated particular places, people, and objects with mysterious healing powers, and then gathered around them. Even the Gospel of John records this human impulse in its description of a pool called Beth-zatha, whose waters were believed to have healing properties. The "blind, lame, and paralyzed" lay nearby, the Gospel records, hoping to reach the pool and be healed when the water was "stirred up" and its powers activated.

Yet, accounts of pilgrimages to sites of healing reveal that we're generally not satisfied with being healed only—we also crave an explanation for the healing. It's not enough that a place, person, or thing *can* heal us; we have a deep human need to know *why*.

Hence, rich tales and legends often accrue around healing pilgrimage sites to explain the curative powers. These tales are as likely to be a mixture of hearsay, conjecture, and pious wishful thinking as they are to be true. The Gospel of John also records our human impulse to explain and understand the mystery. In some versions of that Gospel's manuscripts, an unlikely verse was inserted that ascribes Beth-zatha's healing powers to one of God's angels: "for an angel of the Lord went down at certain seasons into the pool, and stirred up the water; whoever stepped in first after the stirring of the water was made well from whatever disease that person had."

At El Santuario de Chimayó in Chimayó, New Mexico, the healing agent is not water, but dirt. Not just any dirt, but holy dirt drawn from *el posito*, a small hole in the ground in a tiny room just off the sanctuary. Various stories compete to describe the origin of the dirt's healing properties, but the handwritten testimonies of healing, the photographs of the healed, and the no-longer-needed crutches and pros-thetic limbs all left near *el posito* testify to the power itself. This compelling physical evidence of so much faith helps explain why every year on Good Friday, thousands of pil-grims walk from as far away as Albuquerque, some on their knees for part of the journey, and descend upon El Santuario to seek healing and blessings from God.

The National Shrine of Saint Jude in Chicago is the pilgrimage destination for those seeking aid from the "patron saint of seemingly impossible or desperate causes." Until recent decades, Jude was a relatively unknown saint, but those who have received his aid "publish the miracles"— spread the word that Jude can help in even the most desperate situations. Today, those who feel they have nowhere else to turn flood the saint with petitions for restoration of all kinds: physical healing, relief from unemployment, the safe return of sons and husbands from war. The fact that so little is known about Jude himself seems only to endear him more to those seeking his help; he resonates with everyday people in ways that other, more exalted saints, do not. Ironically, the saint's very obscurity has earned him widespread devotion.

At the Healing Rooms of Santa Maria Valley, in Santa Maria, California, healing is not associated with any particular feature of the landscape, sacred object, or holy personality. Quite the contrary. The Healing Rooms' entire ministry is founded on the premise that God can and does use ordinary people in ordinary circumstances to bring healing to those in need. Miracles and healing, they say at the Healing Rooms, can occur anywhere. Yet, paradoxically, the very uniqueness of this everyman and everywoman approach sets the Healing Rooms of Santa Maria Valley apart. Dramatic stories of divine healing have gotten around and compel people from across the country, even the world, to journey there and pray for miracles in the little unassuming white-steepled church.

We travel to healing pilgrimage sites to receive healing of body and soul, to be sure. But the stories we tell reveal that we are also looking for something deeper: meaning and certainty amidst the turmoil of life. Our holy dirt, our shrine of last resort, our prayers for a miracle—do we hope they will be our tangible points of contact with another realm? In our souls, do we hope that healing will allow us momentarily to pierce this veil that keeps us spiritually blind, lame, and paralyzed, and see for ourselves an angel of the Lord stirring the waters?

ONE

The Lourdes
of America

El Santuario de Chimayó
Chimayó, New Mexico

Deep within a small, verdant river valley in northern New Mexico sits a quiet, worn adobe chapel nearly two centuries old. From a certain vantage point, the sanctuary and its environs seem part of some idyllic pastoral scene: well-loved old church in the foreground, rugged mountain in the background, between them contented livestock grazing in green fields beside a lazy river.

Indeed, from appearances, you'd be hard-pressed to guess that El Santuario de Chimayó is not some forgotten rural church, but is rather the destination for hundreds of thousands of pilgrims who journey here every year to seek healing from the holy dirt; that the significance of El Santuario has not dwindled to the mere charm of some historical relic, but rather remains the source of a remarkable power that continues to draw believers with their fervent prayers for restoration of body and spirit.

This power is most evident on Good Friday every year, when the sick, the faithful, and the curious alike descend upon El Santuario *en masse* to pray to God and—culminating the journey—to draw healing dirt from *el posito*, a little hole in the ground near the sanctuary that in shape and proportion resembles a bellybutton dug right into the earth. When you see it for yourself, you might find it curious that a simple hole maybe two feet across and two feet deep could be the central focus of so much faith and devotion. In fact, *el posito* occupies its own tiny room, a sort of Holy of Holies within the church, as if this miniature well—which really does look like a kind of navel in the flat belly of the earth— were a direct and potent line to the center of the world, to the source of spirit, to the power of God. Perhaps this is why, year after year, legions upon legions of pilgrims are drawn to this sanctuary, to this little *el posito*, source of healing, America's own omphalos.

Yet, come to Chimayó and you will soon discover that though visiting *el posito* may be the culmination of the journey, the process of transformation and healing begins long before you get anywhere near the dirt. Change begins with the walk.

In this sense, Chimayó represents a more traditional kind of spiritual pilgrimage than many others in America—one that involves a journey of some hardship as a way of preparing the heart and mind. Many pilgrims to Chimayó start walking from the town of Española, ten miles away, while many others start from Santa Fe (thirty miles). Some begin in Taos to the north (fifty miles); others walk from Albuquerque to the south (ninety miles). A few walk from even farther afield.

While pilgrims visit Chimayó all year long, the annual pilgrimage on Good Friday is a sight to behold. In groups of a dozen or more, whole families together, or in pockets of twos and threes, pilgrims walk down the freeways and back roads of New Mexico. It's a chaotic-looking, beautiful procession: They walk wearing muscle shirts, T-shirts, flannel shirts, fleece pullovers, ratty jeans, pressed khakis. Vets in fatigues wave American flags. Many walk carrying pictures of Jesus or statues of saints; others bear large crosses and crucifixes, some so big it takes two men to carry them. Some chatter amiably, others are quiet, others hold hands and pray. Many sing as they walk. Some in wheelchairs, both manual and motorized, join the walk. Local radio stations broadcast updates for and about the walkers, giving weather updates and alerting motorists to where the pockets of pilgrims are thickest.

As a sign of devotion, some walk barefoot or crawl on their knees for a portion of the journey, which can take a few hours or a few days. Some walk all night. Some pilgrims camp out alongside the road; a few stay at bed and breakfasts along the way. Communities along the pilgrimage route set up support stops, giving total strangers goodies such as oranges, bottled water, homemade burritos—anything that hungry walkers might need for sustenance. Eventually these streams of pilgrims converge onto the two-lane Route 76, the main road into Chimayó, where they flow into one long, marching column of devotion.

As you quickly discover, walking such long distances takes time. It takes patience. It necessarily slows your frenetic everyday technology-driven pace to a much more human rhythm: one foot in front of the other; repeat. The journey is an opportunity to literally walk yourself out of your everyday experience and into a space of the spirit.

Jan, a pilgrimage veteran, said, "For me, the walking is a good time to reflect. I walk with a lot of personal intentions, and I pray for family members."

Jan's friend Kim said, "I walk as a sign of penance and as a time of reflecting on Christ on the cross and his suffering, and I ask for spiritual guidance along the way."

One man was carrying a large, heavy wooden cross over his shoulder. "The cross is an important reminder," he explained. "It's easy for your mind to drift, easy to get a little more social than reflective—and the whole idea is to get reflective and introspective. And when you're carrying the cross, you *know* it's there. It makes you think."

But the walk is even more than a chance for reflection; it's also an opportunity for transformation in itself—a mini-pilgrimage within the larger journey to Chimayó. A woman named Theresa who has been walking for years said, "There's different things you go through. In the night, you really wonder, 'How much further? *Can we do it?*' And then in the morning, when the sun comes up, the sun is your inspiration and you know you can keep on going."

Theresa's companion Eugene agreed. "You're definitely questioning why you're doing it while you're out there walking. It makes you do some soul-searching, and it's a time of sacrifice—you're giving up stuff. You're letting things go."

As they walk, pilgrims encourage one another, look out for one another (cars speeding by present a real danger), and swap stories of healing, previous pilgrimages, and of El Santuario itself. Interestingly, everyone seems to have a different understanding of El Santuario's origins and the specific healing properties of the dirt.

In fact, another thing you discover on the walk is that much of Chimayó's power lies in its very mystery. Although

El Santuario, sometimes referred to more fully as El Santuario de Nuestro Señor de Esquípulas after the crucifix it houses, is a bona fide phenomenon—or perhaps precisely because it is a phenomenon—no one can pin down the exact story of how and why it came to be.

This is certainly not, however, from a lack of stories to choose from. On a Good Friday sometime around 1810, one of these stories goes, a man named Don Bernardo Abeyta was performing ritual penance in the hills near Chimayó when he saw a strange light emanating from the ground. He began to dig with his bare hands and soon uncovered a crucifix six feet tall, which he named El Señor de Esquípulas after a similar crucifix located in Esquípulas, Guatemala. He notified his neighbors and the local priest of his find, and they proceeded with great rejoicing into nearby Santa Cruz where they placed the crucifix on the altar of the church. The next morning, however, the crucifix had vanished, but Don Bernardo found it again back in its hole in the hills of Chimayó. He returned El Señor to the church in Santa Cruz, only to find it missing again the following morning. Once more they returned the crucifix from its hole in Chimayó to the church in Santa Cruz, but the same thing happened yet again, and "by then, everybody understood that El Señor de Esquípulas wanted to remain in Chimayó, and so a small chapel was built" in the location where he was discovered.

Another story has it like this. Although he was very sick, Bernardo Abeyta was tending his sheep in the hills thinking pious thoughts about how much good he could do the world if it were not for his illness. Just then San Esquípula, his patron saint, appeared to him across the way and "beckoned to him." Abeyta "threw off his blankets and hobbled toward the spot" where the apparition had appeared; he knelt there "and immediately he was cured. The news of his miraculous healing spread quickly, and from that time on the sick were brought to the spot where they too were cured immediately. In thanks and devotion to his patron saint, Don Bernardo built a chapel on the spot."

Yet another explanation circumvents El Señor and Don Bernardo altogether, positing that the healing properties of the dirt were recognized by the Tewa Indians, who inhabited the area long before European settlement. It is even suggested that a healing pool of mud was located in the precise location of today's *santuario*, and that the Native Americans rubbed the earth on their bodies (much like today's pilgrims) or consumed it in order to take advantage of its healing powers.

Under normal circumstances, you might find it easy to dismiss elements of these stories as imaginative embellishment, legend, or myth. After all, how could Don Bernardo find a six-foot crucifix in a hole less than three feet deep?

Yet the long walk to Chimayó puts you in a different frame of mind, a head space where you might find yourself looking at such incongruous details not as fantastic tales but rather as something more like a Zen koan: impossibilities that confound the rational mind in order to awaken it to something larger and more *true* than mere facts can convey. The walk encourages a fundamental shift in perception, from seeing the world in strict rational categories, to perceiving it through the lens of *possibility*. The walk is a chance to begin seeing your illnesses through the eyes of hope instead of fear; to see your frailties and failures through the eyes of grace instead of judgment.

You haven't even reached El Santuario, and already the healing has begun.

While you're walking to Chimayó, you generally enjoy the spaciousness of the open road, but the situation changes once you reach your destination. The various courtyards of El Santuario and the surrounding buildings are choked with pilgrims, vendors, tourists, and local kids with the day off from school. Getting into the sanctuary requires special patience as the queue for entrance spills out the door, through the central courtyard, up the walk and around the corner.

But it's worth the wait. When you enter, you are immediately struck by the intimacy of the sanctuary. Unlike, say, the jaw-dropping, awe-inspiring force Gothic cathedrals achieve through sheer magnitude of scale, this is a manageable sacred space. Whitewashed adobe walls, straight-backed wooden pews, wooden crossbeams supporting the ceiling all give it a feel like home; you feel comfortable inside the sanctuary. The lines and corners of the architecture are a little crooked and wobbly; the building has settled into the earth, and somehow you feel invited to settle into the earth, too.

Yet the space is far from austere. The centerpiece is El Nuestro Señor de Esquípulas, the six-foot crucifix reputedly found by Don Bernardo Abeyta, housed just behind the altar in one of five reredos, colorful decorative panels hand-painted in vivid-but-not-garish light greens, pinks, earthy oranges, and water blues. Each of these reredos reaches from floor to ceiling and portrays various angels, saints, and heroes of the faith.

These reredos help create a sacred context supporting the prayers of the faithful. When you walk into the sanctuary, you feel as though you are entering the community of saints and that you are one of the family. Indeed, the reredos, though executed with unmistakable skill and artistry, feel as if they might have been painted by your neighbor. In Chimayó, faith and devotion occur on the personal level;

God is not so much majestic and grand as he is powerful and nearby.

For many, arriving in the sanctuary is just as important as visiting *el posito*. Eugene described the transition from walking toward Chimayó to arriving in the sanctuary itself: "Once you're inside the chapel you just know it's the completion of a journey—*you're there.*" He started to become emotional. "That's when I let everything go, was right there inside the church. And it just felt good. Troubles, problems, anger, whatever—it was time to give it all up and start over."

Like Eugene, many people sit in the pews and pray or kneel at the altar before El Señor de Esquípulas. Some bring rosaries and other objects of devotion to be blessed by a priest standing by. Eventually they rejoin the line of pilgrims, which files past the altar and through a little door on the left of the sanctuary.

As you leave the sanctuary, you turn a corner, duck through a second door, and suddenly find yourself in a tiny room facing the goal of your journey: *el posito*, the little well, the sacred hole in the ground filled with holy dirt.

This is the culmination of hours or days of walking, so although hundreds of people are waiting their turn to visit *el posito*, no one tries to hurry you. One or two other pilgrims may join you in the room, but everyone is reverent;

approaching the hole, everyone understands, is a holy moment.

The dirt is cool and slightly moist to the touch; it has a slightly reddish tint. Inside the hole are a couple of white plastic spoons that many pilgrims use to scoop small amounts of dirt into plastic bags, envelopes, little ceramic vessels, or other containers they bring with them. Some take the dirt with them to bless their homes; others take it to use on ailing family members; others lay it by in case of future illness.

But some pilgrims hope for a miracle on the spot. One man bent down, picked up a handful of the dirt and rubbed it enthusiastically on his wrist, allowing the excess dirt to fall back into the hole. The woman after him stood directly in the hole and rubbed the dirt on her feet eagerly. Another woman with cataracts smeared the dirt right on her eyelids.

None of those three pilgrims seemed to experience a miraculous healing right there, but that didn't dampen the faith of Carmen, who also visited *el posito* that day. "There have been miracles attributed to the healing powers of the holy dirt," she said with conviction. "And you just pray for your own personal miracles and for other people's miracles." Has she ever experienced one of those miracles? "I feel always a renewal of spirit in my faith, and

I see my family healed a little. So sometimes it's my miracle, sometimes it's somebody else's. It's all good."

Not all pilgrims who take the dirt are as certain as Carmen of its effectiveness, but they're willing to suspend their disbelief, if only a little. Pam came from Virginia with her daughter to experience the pilgrimage and to retrieve some of the dirt for her husband, who had recently recovered from a serious health problem. Does Pam think the dirt truly has healing properties? "I don't know," she said. "But I want to believe it. It's certainly worth a try."

Juan, who comes every year, sees the significance of the dirt in larger terms. "I do have faith and I believe that God does wondrous things. But I think it's within each person's faith. I think that God helps those who help themselves, so that when people have the dirt and they really believe they've got the cure for cancer, their body will do what it thinks is right. I call the dirt 'holy placebo.'"

Yet, Juan reflects on the very real ability of the pilgrimage to raise faith and devotion in even the most reluctant pilgrims. "I've seen nonbelievers, you know, straight-out people who were antireligious, who make the trip and they're changed. Even if they don't take on religion, they take on a bit of faith, I believe. They find something that's bigger than their problems, something that's more than themselves."

After visiting *el posito*, you exit through a long narrow anteroom filled with the paraphernalia of devotion. The variety and sheer number of the faith-related objects stuffed into this room boggles the mind. The most striking, and moving, are perhaps the dozens of crutches and canes—even a banged-up, well-used prosthetic arm—left along the wall, presumably by those who no longer needed them after visiting *el posito*. But these objects of devotion take many forms: Painted images of Our Lady of Guadalupe hang on the wall; photographs of loved ones needing healing are propped on shelves; handwritten notes pleading with God for healing and other handwritten notes thanking God for healing lie on tables. Devotional candles flicker; rosaries of all sizes and varieties hang on hooks; there is a black velvet painting of Jesus wearing the crown of thorns. Plastic and ceramic statues of Mary, Jesus, and saints fill shelves. There is a needlepoint replica of da Vinci's *The Last Supper*.

The utter lack of organization, the kitsch mixed with the tasteful, and the obvious history of real pain, devotion, and gratefulness behind each offering confound and humble you. People bring their brokenness and hurt to El Señor and *el posito*, receive healing and hope, and leave with deep gratitude. If you had any doubts about the healing power of the dirt itself, you no longer doubt that there is *some* serious power at work here. You can feel the force of hope at work in this room, and it seems to follow you as you conclude your journey by stepping back out into the courtyard and bright sunlight.

Referring to the objects of devotion left by so many pilgrims, one man concluded, "There's power in that deep kind of faith," and he was right. Whatever condition you came in, when you make a pilgrimage to Chimayó— whether you experience a profound change of perspective or an actual physical miracle—you can scarcely leave El Santuario without a renewed faith in the power of *possibility*, even the possibility of experiencing God's healing power mediated through nothing but the dirt found in a hole in the ground.

TWO

Finding Jude
the Obscure

The National Shrine of Saint Jude
Chicago, Illinois

"If you feel desperation or hopelessness in your life, you have just found a friend," promises an official website of St. Jude devotion, www.stjudenovena.org. And who hasn't experienced just such desperation and hopelessness? It's not surprising that at one time or another, so many people make a literal or figurative "pilgrimage" to commune with Jude, the patron saint of lost causes. It may be an actual physical pilgrimage to his national shrine in a blue-collar neighborhood of South Chicago, or a more metaphorical boundary crossing, as people of all faiths find ways to incorporate devotion to Jude into their spiritual lives. Whatever brings them to Jude—this gentle and compassionate, if somewhat murky, saint—it's always for the same reason: They feel they have nowhere else to turn. Devotion to Jude reminds us that in the end, any kind of pilgrimage is an expression of profound personal vulnerability. We don't leave our comfort zones because we crave adventure, but because we feel we have few options.

Jude has attained a rather astonishing prominence in American Catholicism—so much so, in fact, that many contemporary Catholics don't realize just how recent such devotion is. Although he now has followers all over the world, barely a hundred years ago Jude was a mere blip on the saintly radar—a historical footnote. Not for nothing is he known as "Jude the Obscure"; Jude's life story is remarkable because it's so perfectly unremarkable. He could be, and is, Everyman.

According to legend, Jude Thaddeus (roughly translated to "generous giver of joy") was a kinsman of Jesus' who probably also grew up in Galilee and had a mother named Mary. We don't know much about him, other than that he was one of the original twelve disciples. Tradition holds that he was married and had at least one child, and that he wrote one of the letters in the New Testament. Other than in that letter that bears his name, Jude speaks once in the entire New Testament.

This sketch is not much on which to base a successful and highly specialized devotional cult. How did we get from such sketchy facts to here, when Jude's name is synonymous with miraculous aid in impossible situations? Some people believe that the content of his New Testament epistle, which encourages Christians to persevere in the midst of persecution and martyrdom, has caused people to associate the concept of "desperate cases" with him. He knew a thing or two about desperation: Jude himself was martyred around AD 65.

Although there is some evidence of limited medieval devotion to Jude and more modern Jude cults in Latin America in the nineteenth century, his veneration didn't get off the ground in a major way until the 1920s. Jude came to America through Claretian missionaries who helped establish a modest shrine to him at Our Lady of Guadalupe parish, a largely Mexican-American church in South Chicago. The cult of Jude gained popularity in the late 1920s, with the saint finally assuming pride of place to the right of the church's main altar in 1929.

Devotees feel it's no coincidence that the saint won this enviable position on the eve of the Great Depression; people were about to need Jude as never before. In fact, in South Chicago, folks were already feeling the pinch months before the October crash, since the closing of local steel mills in February of 1929 had put many parishioners out of work. The local priest, Father Tort, estimated that ninety percent of the families in the parish had no regular paycheck. Devotion to Jude offered a ray of hope to people suffering from unemployment and poverty. Individuals began praying to Jude, and word spread throughout the parish that he was a problem-solver, a go-to saint for the downtrodden. By October 28—Jude's feast day, and just one day before the stock market crashed—more than a thousand people crowded around the church, straining to hear the service inside. Considering that no parish in America had so much as a statue of Jude until 1929, this sudden outpouring of affection marked him as an overnight sensation.

But he proved his worthiness time and again to the faithful. Indeed, Jude guided people through the devastations of the Depression and World War II, and then through the less turbulent 1950s and the social and ecclesiastical changes of the 1960s. Kneeling at Jude's altar, it's impossible not to think about all the petitions that have been brought here through the years, primarily by women: wives pleading for employment for their out-of-work husbands in the 1930s, then praying for safety for their soldier sons a decade later. As Robert Orsi recounts in his book, *Thank You, Saint Jude! Women's Devotion to the Patron Saint of Hopeless Causes*, women have often been warriors at the front-lines of prayer to Jude, upholding the saint as a friend in troubled times and crediting him with help in every kind of difficult situation, from childbirth and abusive marriages to failing finances and uncertain health. Jude has long been a friend to the marginalized, offering help to the weary when no one else seems to care.

It's a quiet Sunday afternoon in the National Shrine of Saint Jude on 91st Street in Chicago. Mass at Our Lady of Guadalupe is over, and parishioners file out into the blazing summer sun, shading their eyes after the dim coolness of the church. A few stragglers remain inside, however, their attention turned toward the shrine before them. A statue of Jude stands there expectantly—not a towering or imposing form, but an almost humble figure bathed in artificial light. The statue is smallish and feels dwarfed by the expansive alcove in which Jude is housed—perhaps a visual realization of the obscure saint so often overlooked. His gentle eyes gaze down on his followers as they pray to him to pray for them in turn. The aesthetic effect of the Jude shrine is not to humble these followers by the sheer grandeur of Christ and his saints; it seems instead to invite them into quiet dialogue. Jude is raised above, yes, but not so high that devotees can't feel the communion.

In front of Jude's statue stands a simple altar, adorned with a gilded cloth that reads, *"St. Jude Pray for Us."* This altar is the site of one of the most meaningful transactions of the Jude pilgrimage experience, both for those who come here personally and those who communicate with the Shrine by mail or e-mail: It houses the thousands of prayer petitions that Jude receives. Some of them are collected in the room next door, full of hundreds of small votive candles in red glass holders. Visitors can light a candle and write a message of prayer to Jude; priests collect these petitions several times a year whenever there is a solemn novena (a nine-day recitation of special prayers to the saint). Faithfully placed under the altar, they become part of a complex community of prayers. On the one hand, devotion to Jude remains an intensely personal affair for many people. After all, Jude intervenes for them at the most unguarded times of their lives, and often knows things about them that even their closest friends and family members don't. But on the other hand, when people pray at the Shrine during the novenas, they are really lifting up *all* of the prayers of *all* of the desperate pilgrims who have sought Jude's aid. Pilgrimage to Jude thus intricately blends both intimacy and distance.

Even Jude's own standing reflects this tension. People have made him an object of devotion, of deepest longing and veneration; but at the same time he is merely an intercessor, a conduit, for them to commune with God. Jude negotiates their lives as a trusted mediator between the ineffable and the here-and-now. Like all saints, he pleads individual cases because of his own righteousness and place in heaven. "I am seeing signs that God is listening to you," one man posts online to Jude. Such faith expresses Jude's place in the scheme of things: If it seems impossible that God has the time to hear our individual problems, well, there's always Jude to stand in the gap. The very fact that devotees know so little about him only serves to underscore the point that he exists to bring people closer to God the Father. His way is not obfuscated by charisma or the generous embroidery of hagiographic legend. He's obscure for a purpose: in order to illuminate the way to God.

Those neophytes who aren't sure how to pray to Jude can pick up a prayer card—a simple, laminated, wallet-sized document with an illustration of Jude on the front and a prayer for recitation on the back. After invoking the apostle, this prayer articulates the keening, plaintive wail that wells up in the spirit of the desperate: "Pray for me, I am so helpless and alone." The prayer goes on to request "visible and speedy help where help is almost despaired of," and gives the supplicants space to name the particular trial or problem that has driven them to Jude's door. Devotion to Jude is specific, personal, and highly practical. He's a problem-solver, an entrepreneur, a medical doctor, a relationship expert: in short, a uniquely American saint, perfectly suited for the complex struggles, and deep personal isolation, of modern life.

Jude is the ultimate hand-sold saint; people who pray to him often begin to do so because of the encouragement of a friend or family member. Such recommendations typically come when a person has hit rock bottom and doesn't know where to turn. Other people respond to Jude advertisements they see in the newspaper or on billboards. Consider the case of Henry Green, an African American Chicagoan who found himself unemployed with a wife and five children to support. In 1961, he attended a novena after seeing an ad for it in the newspaper, and decided to pray to Jude. "The fact was that I needed that inner comfort, and wanted to be in a position to help my family," he says. Henry got a Chicago city parks job two months later, and credits his success to the novenas.

Another woman tells of a particular family devotion to the saint. Before she was born, her father was out of work and her parents prayed that he would find a job so that they could get married. In return, they promised that they would name their firstborn child after their saintly benefactor. Since she was a girl, they settled on "Judith," the name a constant reminder of Jude's intervention on their family's behalf.

The decision to name a child after Jude is just one manifestation of what Jude devotees call "publishing the miracle";

whenever Jude performs a miracle on someone's behalf, that person is obliged to spread the message of Jude's aid far and wide. ("I promise, O blessed St. Jude, to be ever mindful of this great favor, to always honor you as my special and powerful patron, and to gratefully encourage devotion to you," concludes the basic Jude prayer.) For the Jude devotee, then, praying the prayer and even receiving the hoped-for deliverance is not the end of the pilgrimage journey. Jude devotion stresses the importance of making other people aware of the ways Jude has helped us. Only a few years ago, this was often done in the classified ads of local newspapers. In between the announcements of cars for sale and pets for adoption would be the powerful words, "Thank you, St. Jude!" before an anonymous devotee praised Jude for healing a broken relationship or otherwise making a way out of no way.

The most famous example of "publishing the miracle" comes from the entertainer Danny Thomas, who struggled so much in his early career that he prayed to Jude, promising that if the saint would prosper his career (which must have seemed unlikely at the time, as Thomas had all of seven dollars to his name and no prospects), Thomas would erect a shrine to Jude. The saint came through and so did Thomas, who began in the 1950s to raise money for a Memphis children's hospital that would be devoted to finding cures for devastating diseases such as leukemia. This would be no ordinary shrine, but an ongoing major medical facility with a commitment that would make Jude proud. By finding treatments and even cures for these diseases, St. Jude Children's Research Hospital would continue "publishing the miracle" by offering hope in Jude's name. One miraculous fact is that since the hospital opened in the early 1960s, it has never had to charge any pediatric patients beyond what was covered by their own insurance. Children with no health insurance are treated for free. One can imagine that this ministry to the hopeless, the poor, and the infirm would thrill the heart of the enigmatic saint.

Certainly, not every person who has been on the receiving end of Jude's help has been as visible about proclaiming it as Danny Thomas, with his high-profile fundraising efforts and repeated public recitals of his Jude story. However, the Internet has taken the public announcement of gratitude to the saint to a whole new level, and expanded the network of thanksgiving. As Jude devotion has gone hi-tech, people post messages of thanks on websites both official and unofficial. For example, "Mike," an anxious father, thanked Jude online for the miraculous recovery of his nine-year-old son, who was paralyzed for a week in the ICU for no discernible reason. After neurological tests were inconclusive, the boy began walking one day on his own. "I turned to you in one of the darkest moments in my life and prayed with all my heart," Mike wrote. "You showed me once again why you are a powerful patron saint of hopeless cases. God bless you and thank you for shining your light in my son's life."

Sometimes, people acknowledge Jude's intervention even without concrete evidence of any miracle. Jennifer writes from England, posting on the official St. Jude novena website that "although I haven't, as yet, had a positive answer, I really felt his presence. He definitely heard me, and I feel much better." For these people, Jude's spiritual accompaniment is as important, if not more important, than any visible marvel he might perform.

Jude is clearly one saint for whom the physical and tangible are less significant than the spiritual and emotional. On this score, we learn a good deal about Jude by comparing him to other saints. Consider, for example, that there are no attested relics of Jude, no bones or hair or possessions that tie him to a particular place. His National Shrine in Chicago, as well as shrines in Baltimore, San Francisco, Rome, and other cities, are wonderful places to visit but aren't considered necessary in order to feel close to Jude. He lives everywhere and nowhere, and as such, pilgrims can pray to him wherever they are (though some followers do feel that petitions made at his Chicago shrine will have the greatest chance of success). There are but few celebrated moments in history attributed to Jude: an isolated vision here, a miraculous artistic icon there. Journalist Liz Trotta calls him the "guerilla" saint, working behind the scenes and always just out of sight: "he arrives as an anonymous holy helper, a bulge in the curtain. The impalpability of Jude is the essence of his appeal."

This makes a Jude "pilgrimage" as slippery and ambiguous as the saint himself. For every pilgrim who comes to this relatively modest shrine in Chicago, there are thousands of others who will never make the trip, but who feel inseparably connected to Jude through prayer and ritual. Some do prefer to commune with Jude at the Shrine. One Chicago woman, for instance, explains that she would rather say her prayers at the parish than pray alone at home. "Father will give a little sermon, and we have benediction. It's a very nice feeling to be gathered together in a group like this, and to see so many people who have faith in St. Jude." But for the most part, the pilgrimage is interior and spiritual; Jude can easily be an armchair saint, and is characteristically accommodating of our circumstances.

Perhaps that's because of his unique mission: As the patron saint of lost causes, needy people, desperate cases, and the like, Jude bends over backward to make his veneration easy for people who hardly need one more difficulty in their lives.

It's likely that every spiritual pilgrim will have just cause, at some point or another, to call upon Jude. And while it's excellent to visit the National Shrine and soak up its atmosphere of decades of Judean devotion with other like-minded souls, Jude would be just as happy to connect with us at our kitchen tables or on our front porches, one on one. Finding Jude, then, is a pilgrimage of the heart rather than the arduous pilgrim journey of yesteryear: We travel inward, acknowledging the deep recesses of desperation, isolation, and anxiety that reside in the human heart. And then we pray.

"Most holy apostle, St. Jude, faithful servant and friend of Jesus . . ."

THREE

Love Is in Itself Healing

The Healing Rooms of the Santa Maria Valley
Santa Maria, California

I n Santa Maria, a nondescript mid-sized city on California's central coast, a small, unassuming white-steepled church has become an internationally renowned hotbed of divine healing. Yet those pilgrims seeking healing at these "Healing Rooms," though they may have traveled from across North America or from across the globe, might easily drive right on by the place, since the only indications that they've arrived are a hand-painted sign and a modest banner slung off the eaves in the church's green, manicured courtyard.

The Healing Rooms of the Santa Maria Valley aren't officially affiliated with the church whose building they use on weekdays. They are a separate ministry, a member of the

International Association of Healing Rooms based in Spokane, Washington, a group dedicated to a "common vision to establish healing back into the body of Christ." They take their inspiration from Mark 16:17-18: "And these signs will accompany those who believe . . . they will lay their hands on the sick, and they will recover." There are literally hundreds of Healing Rooms affiliated with this organization scattered across the globe, as close to home as the United States and Canada and as far flung as France, Holland, Zambia, India, Korea, and Singapore.

Each of the Healing Rooms belonging to the International Association of Healing Rooms operates under the same basic principles, so you might expect them to be roughly interchangeable; why should the Healing Rooms in Ashtabula, Ohio, be any different from the Healing Rooms in Anchorage, Alaska? Yet the word has gotten out that the Healing Rooms of the Santa Maria Valley are particularly effective, even among its fellow Healing Rooms.

"They have this amazing track record for people with cancer getting healed," said Roger, pastor of a church several hundred miles away. "There are other Healing Rooms closer by, but that one in particular was experiencing miracles. That's why we took Phil there."

Phil was a member of Roger's church, the drummer in the praise band. "He was really sick," Roger continued. "Down to 110 pounds; he couldn't walk without help; he wasn't eating. He was doing chemo. . . . The doctors had given him a month to live at that point. We were desperate, and we heard about the Healing Rooms in Santa Maria."

As many pilgrims who set out to seek healing know, a disease or disability can make the pilgrimage journey itself especially challenging. Roger's trip with Phil was no exception. "It took everything we had just to get him up there because of his condition," Roger said. The leaders of the Healing Rooms are aware of the difficulties many visitors experience just getting there, and they do everything they can to accommodate travelers, including serving their practical needs. They post airline, bus, and car rental information on their website. They arrange for local hotels to give discounts for visitors to the Healing Rooms. They even operate on a traveler-friendly schedule: They're open four times a week, on Monday nights and Tuesday mornings, and again on Wednesday nights and Thursday mornings, so visitors can squeeze in two prayer sessions during a single two-day trip. Roger took advantage of this schedule on his trip with Phil. "We did the whole thing: We went up during the day, got prayer that evening, stayed overnight in a hotel, went back for prayer the next morning and came home that afternoon."

Traditional pilgrimages of healing are often associated with a specific geographic location, such as Lourdes in

France; or a sacred object, such as the dirt in Chimayó, New Mexico; or with a particular site dedicated to a holy personality, such as the Shrine of St. Jude in Chicago. The Healing Rooms of the Santa Maria Valley have a different approach. It is true that these Healing Rooms in particular draw pilgrims from far and wide (the pilgrims often eschew other Healing Rooms closer to home just to travel to Santa Maria), but the leaders are quick to tell you that their "amazing track record," as Roger put it, has nothing to do with some holy relic they possess or some charismatic personality they have on staff. In fact, it's quite the opposite; it's their focus on God alone as the source of healing, they believe, that sets them apart. It's the manner of their praying that lets the healing flow.

Trudy drove all day to make it to the Healing Rooms in time for prayer on Monday evening. Her first stop was in the office to fill out a brief questionnaire describing the nature of her need and whether she had ever visited the Healing Rooms before. One entire wall of the office was wallpapered from floor to ceiling with the testimonies of people who have received healing here—a silent but powerful witness to the Healing Rooms' confident claim, "Jesus still heals today!" When she finished the questionnaire, Trudy waited in the "soaking room" until she was called for her time of prayer.

Many pilgrimages include a period of quiet contemplation, a time of preparation for the moment of contact with the holy that is about to occur. The soaking room serves this purpose at the Healing Rooms. It is a waiting room, but it is much more; it's where the visitor can relax and "soak up the presence of the Lord," as one volunteer put it, and so become primed for the prayer session itself. Indeed, the soaking room does feel saturated with a peaceful spirit. The chairs that line the walls are cushy and comfortable. Inspirational art reminds visitors of words of hope and healing they will find in the Bible. Soft music plays gently. The half-dozen people who are likely to be sharing the soaking room at a given time are drawn into themselves and quiet—save those who begin crying. For them, plenty of tissue boxes are scattered about on chairs and on windowsills.

After a time, a volunteer appeared at the inner door, gently announced Trudy's name, and escorted her deeper into the building. Only the office and the soaking room are dedicated for use by the Healing Rooms; every other room the ministry uses is borrowed during the week from the host church. So, in contrast to the near-luxurious comfort of the soaking room, the prayer sessions themselves are conducted in functional Sunday school classrooms furnished with relatively uncomfortable chairs. Paper rainbows and cut-out Jesuses adorn the bulletin boards in some rooms; in others, children's toys lie scattered in the corners.

But this step down in comfort doesn't seem to dampen the spirits of the volunteers, who work in teams of two or three for the prayer sessions. Trudy's team began by asking her the nature of her need. As is true for most pilgrimages, people come seeking prayer for all kinds of things: for physical healing of ailments and diseases, of course, but also for healing in broken relationships and even broken finances. As one woman put it, "They'll pray for *anything* for you there." Usually the volunteers read, or recite from memory, passages from the Bible *à propos* to the visitor's situation. Trudy had come for emotional healing of some deep-seated hurts and psychological pain.

After a time of discussing Trudy's issues, one of the volunteers asked if she was ready for prayer. Both volunteers then gently laid their hands on Trudy's shoulders and head and commenced with prayer. Their prayers were vocal and strong. "I thank you, Lord, for Trudy," they prayed, "and ask right now in the name of Jesus that you deliver her from her affliction, her fears, from the damage done to her many years ago." As he prayed, the lead volunteer began to receive mental images, and he shared them with Trudy. "I see wings," he said, his eyes closed. "I see you with wings, and they are new and strong—and you are learning to use them, and I see you rising up! Thank you, Jesus."

The style and content of the prayers vary according to the personality and particular gifts of the person praying. The next morning, Trudy returned for a second prayer session, this time with a team led by a seemingly fragile, mild-mannered older woman whose prayers were compassionate but surprisingly *tough*. "I command the spirit of loneliness and rebellion to come out of Trudy, *right now*! In the name of *Jesus*!" she shouted, while gently rubbing Trudy's sternum and stomach—the spot where Trudy had identified the physical manifestation of her suffering. "Are you okay, honey?" the volunteer paused and asked Trudy, and then returned to commanding loneliness and rebellion to leave Trudy's life, immediately, once and for all. Throughout the session, Trudy responded to the prayers emotionally with weeping, shaking, yelling, and violent coughing. By the end of the session, Trudy had found an emotional release that left her laughing from relief and joy. Later, she found it difficult to talk about the session. She felt changed and healed, she said, and she was grateful for the relief she had found—yet it was an intensely personal experience. She also acknowledged that the nature of the issues that had brought her to the Healing Rooms was complex, and would require ongoing prayer and healing.

Just as many pilgrimages involve a time of preparation before the moment of encounter, many also involve a time of decompression afterward. Trudy certainly needed this, so she returned to the soaking room in order to reflect on and integrate the experience she'd just had before getting in her car and driving back home.

The prayers that occur in the Healing Rooms of the Santa Maria Valley have a definite charismatic edge, but the volunteers themselves come from over thirty churches in the area, some of which have a strong charismatic tradition, such as Foursquare and Vineyard fellowships, and others not so much, such as Presbyterian and Roman Catholic churches. Yet there is no discussion of doctrinal or denominational differences in the Healing Rooms. This unity-in-diversity itself makes a lasting impression on visitors. One man said, "There, it's not about pushing or pulling, saying, 'It's only Catholics' or 'It's only Lutherans.' It doesn't make any difference what our backgrounds are—it's about the relationship we have with our Lord. And that's what's going to save our world one of these days."

Some people come wholeheartedly expecting to be healed right on the spot, and that's exactly what some people say they get. Gladys was out shopping when "my heart started acting up," she said. "My heart skips a beat, and I had been taking medication to try to get it to beat regular, and my heart would almost just come *out* of me when I had those kinds of attacks. And this was the worst attack I ever had. I was very, very weak." She went home to lie down, but the episode didn't pass. "I told my husband, 'I need to go to the emergency.' But I also wanted to go to the Healing Rooms, and I thought, 'They keep you so long at the emergency that by the time I get out, the Healing Rooms will be closed!' So I decided to go to the Healing Rooms first to have prayer, then if I wasn't healed, I would go on over to the emergency."

Pilgrimages generally aren't so spur-of-the-moment as this, but why should a spontaneous, even emergency pilgrimage, be any less effective? Call it an *acute* pilgrimage.

Gladys's husband drove her to the Healing Rooms in a hurry. "As I passed the soaking room," she said, "I felt the Spirit of the Lord come out of the soaking room. We walked a few steps further, and I told my husband, 'I'm healed!'" How did she know she was healed? As she sat in the soaking room a few minutes later, waiting for her time of prayer, "I was just at peace. A wonderful peace. And I knew that I was healed because all the weakness had gone away, and the pounding of my heart was gone." Some time later she did go see a doctor. "And he said to me, 'Do you have a pacemaker?' and I said, 'No!' And he said, 'Well, I wish my heart was as good as yours.'" Gladys paused, then added, "It's been quite a number of years, and it's still healed."

Another time, Gladys went to the Healing Rooms for prayer concerning a cataract in her right eye. "I didn't feel anything different at the time," she says. "But then I went to my doctor appointment, and the doctor just kept digging in my right eye, and I stopped him and said, 'Is there something wrong?' And he realized he was losing his composure because he was bent right down over my eye, digging in every direction, and he said, 'You had two cataracts—two different kinds!—and I can't find either of them.' So I was healed again."

Gladys talks freely about being "healed," but the leaders of the Healing Rooms are careful about the terminology they use. A "miracle," in Healing Rooms lingo, is a spontaneous, instantaneous remission of a particular condition, such as what Gladys experienced with her heart and cataracts. "Healing," on the other hand, is progressive and may take days, weeks, months, or longer. Stories of "miracles" may be dramatic, but stories of "healing" are just as compelling.

Jonathan sought out the Healing Rooms of the Santa Maria Valley because, he said, "I had been diagnosed with hepatitis C. I had no energy whatsoever. Just to get up and come downstairs was a battle, or to put on my clothes, or anything. Then I was rushed to the hospital because I was throwing up blood. The doctors told me my liver was beyond any kind of treatment they could offer. They said either I'd die, or I'd need a liver transplant."

"I was in a battle for my life," he said, but his own faith community, despite good intentions, wasn't helping him very much. "It's funny, when you're near death, you become awake to the way people really are. And I had some good Christians who came to see me, but I said, 'I don't want that person to come over here because I can see they're walking with a bunch of *sympathy*! You can see death in their eyes. I even had a pastor tell me how somebody he knew had the same thing and *died*. It's like, Hey! Thanks a lot!'"

Jonathan found a different attitude at the Healing Rooms. "The love there is contagious. It's an awesome environment because it's an atmosphere of love. It's the real thing, it's not make-believe. It opens people up and prepares them to receive what God has for them when it comes to their healing. It's a very powerful time with people who really do contend with you for your healing." Jonathan reports that he returned again and again to the Healing Rooms. "I continued for years contending for my healing and wondering why it took so long for me. I went through all the things you imagine you might go through if you were given a death sentence." At a certain point, though, "I noticed some improvement, and I just continued to improve, and it was finally the end of the nightmare." One year later, Jonathan reports that he is still healed of hepatitis C and is now full of energy.

Jonathan repeatedly emphasized, as do the Healing Rooms, that the Healing Rooms work with "divine healing, not faith healing." The difference is significant. "If this was faith healing," said Jonathan, "you'd end up thinking, 'Maybe my faith is not enough.'" Divine healing, by contrast, is rooted in "the healing power of Jesus" which the Healing Rooms literature says can "destroy the works of the devil, cancer; fibromyalgia, tumors, diabetes, blindness, chronic pain," and more. "We have high expectations here," said one of the leaders.

This is good news for those who may leave the Healing Rooms feeling the same as they came. "We heard Santa Maria is experiencing a real big movement of miracles right now," said Marvin, one of a group of men who had flown in from Chicago for prayer. "The Healing Rooms are all over the place, we've even got a couple by us. But this is where it's happening; here in Santa Maria is where God is working. I came and asked for physical healing in my hand and back. I still have the physical manifestations, but that doesn't mean that God doesn't heal gradually. I was expecting healing. I'm still expecting it."

Marvin's comment that "this is where it's happening . . . where God is working" underscores a tension inherent in the Healing Rooms' theology: If God is the source of the healing, and God is everywhere, why should Marvin have to board a plane to seek out that healing? Other pilgrimage sites avoid this question by focusing on the uniqueness of their site; what they have, you can't get at home. But why did Marvin have to embark on this pilgrimage to find the very same God he worshiped at home?

Marvin's friend Alex, who had come with him from Chicago, had a pragmatic response to this question. "I keep hearing stories of healing and God's power and the love being poured out here in Santa Maria, and I have a hunger for that. So I thought, instead of forcing God to come to me, I figured I'd go check him out. I would like to think that I can get whatever God is doing just by sitting at home on my couch, but that isn't necessarily the case." Alex indicated that making the effort to come on pilgrimage was itself a kind of signal to God that he meant business. "If I want to get hold of God in a powerful way, it may mean leaving home, it may mean leaving my comfort zone, whatever that is—geographic, spiritual, emotional."

Although the Healing Rooms of the Santa Maria Valley don't boast, say, a unique spring with special healing waters or a proprietary saint to intercede on behalf of the pilgrim, Alex did discover one thing that made this pilgrimage destination unique: the lack of ego among the volunteers.

"They make an effort to take themselves out of the equation and just be channels of God's love. So it's very encouraging to know that I don't have to get the 'right guy' or the 'superstar Christian' in order to get healed. Here, the focus is on Christ. The Lord is using sittin'-in-the-pews everyday people here," he adds, "so there are no big names here."

The Healing Rooms intentionally cultivate this selfless approach by beginning with a worship service for the volunteers, a transitional time that allows them to leave behind their own cares and become focused on the ministry at hand. On the day the group of men from Chicago visited, twenty or so volunteers gathered in the church's gymnasium (a shuffleboard court is laid into the green tile on the floor) for a time of prayer and worship. The group from Chicago was also invited to join. A small worship team led the group in song with a guitar, a hand drum, and other small instruments. Everyone stood in a large circle and sang; some entered the center of the circle and danced; one or two danced and waved multicolored banners resembling butterflies.

When the music ended, the group entered a time of prayer. One volunteer prayed over the group from Chicago and shared a vision for them: "I saw a fire on a map—you know, like that map at the beginning of *Bonanza*—a fire starting in Canada and spreading down through the Great Lakes, a fresh fire of revival . . . so get ready for it!"

Alex found the words spoken over him and his friends were encouraging and healing in their own way. "I was given a thought of assurance that God knows me and loves me, and that he's got good plans for me. So I was very touched. The physical stuff is fantastic, but for me the spiritual and emotional components were much more what I was hoping for, and that's what I got."

Still others travel to the Healing Rooms not knowing what to hope for at all. "We weren't even sure what to expect," said Roger about his first trip to the Healing Rooms with Phil, the cancer-ridden drummer in the praise band. "For a long time before that he was pretty hopeless about any kind of change. We thought, 'If this helps at all to relieve some of his pain, we would be more than happy.'"

"At the time, nothing miraculous happened," Roger said, "yet it was a marked point; he was much more positive after visiting the Healing Rooms. And then we saw an incredible remission of cancer so that he was back on his feet again. He didn't stop doing the treatments, but the doctors were like, 'This is *unbelievable*' because they had literally given him a month to live. And now he was going in the other direction."

The effects of Phil's remission rippled beyond Phil's own life and underscored a recurring theme surrounding the Healing Rooms of the Santa Maria Valley: the genuine love the volunteers have for those they pray for. "I was really moved by the way they treated people and the way God seems to use their ministry in a powerful way," said Roger. "That was the journey that opened my mind to understand what they do and how they do it."

Phil's remission was remarkable but, unfortunately, temporary. "By the end of the year, Phil was back to work. He had gained thirty pounds, he was walking again, he was driving again. He was basically functioning normally," said Roger. "But then in the spring of the next year, he started to experience headaches. He went again to get tests, and they found a spot on his brain. The cancer had spread from his back to his brain and it continued to spread very quickly. By the summer he was bedridden again, and he passed away in the fall."

What does Roger, a pastor, make of that—Phil's apparent divine healing and sudden relapse? "In my mind there is no real explanation that completely satisfies anybody, even myself, why God completely heals some people and why he doesn't others. But I think Phil understood that there was this grace of God that you've been given 'X' amount of time to live your life and enjoy it, and Phil was given a big miracle."

Though the cancer ultimately claimed Phil's life, helping Phil through his ordeal has had lasting repercussions through Roger's own life, and now Roger goes to the

Healing Rooms for prayer several times a year, often for no particular reason other than to feel supported, cared for, and loved. "I've been around other prayer ministries where it's been strange, or a little bit contrived or forced, but I never feel that when I go to the Healing Rooms. The most striking thing about them is the incredible love they have for God and for the people they minister to. And a lot of the words they've spoken to me have been words of affirmation, and I feel God's affirmation. That's been very helpful and releasing. It's been empowering. It hasn't changed my situation per se, but it has changed my perspective about the direction of my life. So there has been a kind of inner healing. The volunteers reiterate again and again, it's all about love, and they administer the love of God to people. That in itself is healing."

PART II

Pilgrimages of
Benedictine Hospitality

"When you go on retreat, you're going there so you can pursue God in a new way," says Steve Pollick, a longtime pilgrim to the Abbey of Gethsemani in Kentucky. His observation explains a good deal about the relationship of retreat and pilgrimage. A retreat is a specific form of pilgrimage; there is an intentionality to the retreat experience that elevates it from being a mere holiday—"getting away from it all" for a few days—to a chrysalis, a potential site of lasting spiritual transformation.

Retreatants are pilgrims on both an internal and an external journey. Certainly, going on retreat highlights the notion that a traditional pilgrimage involves a physical journey to an actual place and a sacrifice of something on the part of the pilgrim. In medieval times, that sacrifice—the word literally means "to make holy"—often involved the surrender of physical comforts on a long, awkward, and even perilous journey. Nowadays, danger is downplayed and even discomfort is rare, but the pilgrim retreat demands another kind of sacrifice, a temporary surrender of the commodity perhaps most highly prized by moderns: time. In turn, this sacrifice of time opens the door for transformation and renewal, the inner journey any pilgrim craves.

For a retreat to be a spiritual pilgrimage, it needs to happen in a place where the hosts understand this dynamic of sacrifice and create space for pilgrims to worship and to confront the reality of their lives. When we set out to write this book, we did not consciously choose only Benedictine retreat centers; we knew we wanted to include several retreat experiences and naturally gravitated toward these three, which all happen to be Benedictine.

An accident? We don't think so. All three places are grounded in a unique history of receiving pilgrims, a history that stretches back 1,500 years. It's unusual for any system of government to last for 1,500 years. Unheard of, even. But that is the case with the Rule of Saint Benedict, a brief document written in the early sixth century to govern both the spiritual and the earthly standards of monastic life. Benedict's sense of order, and his gentle but firm instructions for how to keep a monastery humming, are still in practice in hundreds of monastic communities today.

A Benedictine monastery provides a consummate experience of Christian hospitality, making it an attractive destination for weary pilgrims. As Benedict wrote so long ago, "Let all guests who arrive be received as Christ, because He will say: 'I was a stranger and you took Me in.' And let due honor be shown to all, especially to those 'of the household of the faith' and to wayfarers." Any pilgrim who has arrived at the doorstep of a Benedictine community will understand when we say that it is often the perfect place to find rest and spiritual renewal. However, this connotes more than just a cordial reception of guests. The word "hospitality," in fact, derives from the same Latin root that engendered the words "hospital" and "hospice"—with their accompanying meaning of healing the sick. Benedictine monasteries are places of healing, balms of Gilead where the broken soul can find wholeness.

In addition to their famed hospitality, Benedictine monasteries and retreat centers often invite pilgrims to participate in their extraordinary worship life, also patterned after the Rule. In it, Benedict outlined a regimented daily rhythm of brief services, or offices, centered on the chanting of the psalms. Some monasteries have modernized the worship in one way or another—either condensing the offices from the original seven or eight into a more manageable four or five, or singing in the vernacular instead of in Latin—but their daily heartbeat is still regulated by the methodical ancient pacemaker that is the Divine Office.

One interesting and surprising facet of the chapters that follow is that although all three retreat centers follow in the tradition of Saint Benedict, only one of them is actually Roman Catholic—the Abbey of Gethsemani in Kentucky. Although some Catholics are members of the Community of Jesus on Cape Cod, it has an ecumenical identity and spans the denominational spectrum. In all, it's comprised of several hundred people who commit themselves to living out the principles of Benedict's Rule in the modern world. Finally, Mt. Calvary retreat center is run by an order of Episcopal brothers, but it too draws upon the ancient principles that Benedict articulated. In all three cases, people of any faith are welcome to make a retreat, and are invited to join the monastics in the peaceful daily round of rest and worship.

FOUR

Safe House

*The Community of Jesus
Cape Cod, Massachusetts*

The best kept secret in Massachusetts may well be the Community of Jesus, an ecumenical Christian community located just at the inner elbow of Cape Cod. It's not a monastery, exactly. Although its character is Benedictine and its worship life is prescribed by the daily ritual of the Divine Office, it's neither Protestant nor Catholic, and its celibate brothers and sisters (who are not usually referred to as monks or nuns) are joined by other Community members who are called "householders" and have families and jobs in the workaday world. But a monastic air adheres to this unusual place, where about three hundred full-time members (including brothers, sisters, and householders) have managed to carve out an unexpected slice of heaven on the rocky shoals of the Cape. Outlanders who come here, either as admiring but casual visitors or pilgrims in search of the unmistakably spiritual quality that seems to permeate the very air, can't help being changed by this place. That sacred essence extends from a rare commitment to honesty, on both an individual and communal level, and to spiritual vulnerability as a catalyst to growth and astonishing creativity.

For pilgrims who have visited other monasteries, it's rather surprising to see how young, how vital, the sisters and brothers are here. In an era when Catholic and Anglican vocations have mourned a nosedive in the number of young applicants, the Community of Jesus' convent and friary are filled with many in their twenties and thirties. To be sure, a fair number of the more than eighty brothers and sisters are middle-aged or older, but the general sensibility is one of zest and vigor. One twenty-something sister, for example, cheerfully exclaims "Awesome!" after hearing a spot of good news.

That youthful energy extends through the rest of the community as well, which welcomed five newborns in 2004 and features many young families as well as older couples. One extraordinary feature of community life is that householders generally share a home. Rather than adhering to the American gold standard of the single-family household, members of the Community of Jesus favor the multi-family home, where people share chores and responsibilities. (Finances are kept separate for each biological family.) The concept behind this is that by living together, Christians can more fully internalize the ideal of bearing one another's burdens. The arrangements can lead to some unusual mixings, with many generations living together. It's also not atypical here for teenagers to live for a time with people other than their parents. They still see their parents every day at church and other activities, but the experience of living with other people teaches them valuable lessons in independence, consideration, and responsibility.

Those who come here on pilgrimage enjoy some of the fruits of this lifestyle in a "trickle-down" effect, as the values that Community members live at home enable them to reach out in ministry to those who visit. It's not always easy for Community members to live in close quarters, especially since they place a high premium on honesty and openness. One visitor was surprised to find, when he had lunch with a Community household, that a man who lived there was being told some hard truths about his conduct in a very public way at the table. The visitor was even more surprised to realize that the fellow took this mealtime correction in stride; Community members are expected to speak the truth to one another in love. They can then resume the relationship, which is improved by this honest airing of problems.

Such honesty, members feel, is key to understanding not only life in the Community but the Christian walk more broadly defined.

That same lunchtime visitor, for example, had been wondering how a small group with 300-odd members could possibly have created the vibrant arts community that centers around the Church of the Transfiguration (discussed below). When he witnessed the gentle but firm rebuke that took place that afternoon, he had an epiphany about the source of the Community's unparalleled artistic creativity: It is made possible by unmasked honesty. John French, one of the Community's retreat directors, explains that most of us expend a vast amount of energy simply maintaining the masks we show to the world. We strive to be viewed as attractive and financially stable, in control of our emotions and aces in our jobs. We aim for people to see us as good parents, whether or not we are, and feel exposed when our children have a knack for bringing out our less savory selves. But at the Community, says John, people see each other warts and all, the net result being "that all the creative energy that has been utilized to keep the real you hidden and under control is set free." It's perfectly amazing, he says, how much animation and strength can be released when people are willing to lay down the mask of perfection and experience God's love.

This honesty is not just for full-time Community members. People who are on a spiritual journey of any kind will find that one of the most significant aspects of any genuine pilgrimage is self-confrontation. For some people, the romantic image of pilgrimage is that pilgrims are simultaneously running toward a holy place and fleeing difficult aspects of their past. But the past has a way of finding us wherever we go; we cannot hide from ourselves and expect to experience spiritual growth. What's important in the pilgrimage process is to find a safe house, a place where we can lay all our cards on the table without shocking ourselves or anyone else who has come to rely upon the façade we present to the world.

The Community of Jesus is such a place. Dave Krueger, a businessman who began visiting the Community in the early 1970s and is now an "oblate" (someone who has covenanted to live in the Spirit of The Community's *Rule of Life* but does not live there full-time), says that this quality of refuge is what affected him most strongly in his initial visits. "There are very few safe environments where you can hang out your dirty laundry and people hold your confidence," he explains. "There's an extraordinary fiduciary quality of the people at the Community of Jesus, and a basic respect for human dignity. In our society of American individualism, weakness is not an especially prized commodity." He particularly appreciates how conflict is handled, citing a rule in Community life that no member can discuss another member unless that person is present. "If I started talking about a third person to you, your job would be to take me to that person and air the complaint directly," he says. "Can you imagine how gossip and backbiting would be eliminated if other churches followed that example?"

The honesty that is lived here filters down to affect the lives of those who visit, even if they are only here for a few days. John French and a fellow retreat director, his wife, Mary, say that pastors in particular often feel liberated by their stay, since as congregational leaders they sometimes feel they must model perfection. This burden of presumed spiritual flawlessness and accomplishment can be wearisome, so it's no wonder that ministers and many others find sanctuary here. "This is a safe place, and there's such a freedom in that," says Mary. "Maybe it's a biblical city of refuge, not because you're just escaping, but because it's a place where you can be honest and yourself."

Let's be clear: There is no agenda for retreats at the Community of Jesus, and pilgrims are not put on any kind of fault-finding display. Rather, those who desire it can get private daily spiritual direction (included in the cost of a retreat) from the retreat directors, who will usually meet with all guests at the beginning of their stay to determine what their desires and goals are for the retreat. Some people decide that this one conversation is enough, and then pursue a more solitary retreat that may include journaling, walking, and praying the Liturgy of the Hours in the Church of the Transfiguration. Others crave more intense guidance. One woman who came on retreat initially requested an hour of spiritual direction every day, but she and the directors increased that when it became clear that she had major problems that required attention and prayer. Whatever a retreatant's spiritual needs may be, individuals at the Community will do what they can to see that those needs are met.

This commitment holds true not just for spiritual direction but for just about every aspect of guests' welfare at the Community. The retreat experience at Bethany House, a lovely older home overlooking the harbor, is comfortable, even luxurious. Soft towels, fresh flowers, fine china, careful attention to detail—these are the finishing touches to visitors' time at Bethany House, where the sisters make guests feel so special that they might reasonably imagine themselves in a friendlier-than-usual Swiss hotel. However, the guestmistress is quick to caution potential visitors that "this is not a bed-and-breakfast. People do need to come for a religious reason." In fact, the very hospitality that is practiced here is an extension of the Community's religious convictions and grounding in the Rule of St. Benedict. In that sixth-century instruction for monastic living, Benedict taught monks that they must receive every guest as they would Christ himself. At Bethany House, that guideline is honored every time a sheet is tucked or a pillow plumped for a guest's comfort.

It is also realized in the immense care taken with guests' meals. While other retreat centers often adopt a necessarily institutional approach to meals, offering a cafeteria or buffet-style menu three times a day, the food at Bethany House is always an occasion. Guests take their meals in a sumptuous dining room with a curving bow window overlooking Rock Harbor. The food itself is almost sinfully epicurean, prepared with the finest ingredients, fresh herbs, and fruits in season. "The sisters who take care of the cooking truly have a passion for it," says Sister Agnes, who helps to serve the guests. "They love to cook for people, and it's a joy to be able to do that." Sister Agnes says she derives pleasure from utilizing the rather vast array of china at Bethany House ("every plate has a story associated with it," she remarks), and in making the place settings beautiful and memorable. "It's something that we know people don't experience a lot in their everyday lives. I love setting tables, and trying to make it unique every time. I know it's a blessing to people."

Rooms at Bethany House are plush and comfortable, furnished with antiques and tasteful art. Each room comes equipped with all the items guests need to make tea, instant coffee, or hot chocolate, including delicate china cups and silver teaspoons. As a testimony to the retreat house's serene character, even the room names are theological: Trinity, Angel, Cross, Compassion, and Grace. Renovations in recent years have ensured that every guest room now has a private bath. There are also two charming reading alcoves on the second floor, one with a built-in window seat.

While the rooms at Bethany House are beautiful and downright sybaritic as retreat quarters go, there are only five of them. So in 2005, the Community began work on Paraclete House, a larger retreat facility that should be finished in 2007. Paraclete House—named after the Greek word for the Holy Spirit, or "comforter," used by Jesus in John 14—will have fourteen rooms and enough beds for eighteen guests, as well as a dining room that can seat up to five hundred people. The large dining facility is an important consideration for Community gatherings and receptions. As with most Community building projects, a good deal of the labor is being done by members themselves.

Why the new construction? As Mary French explains it, the Community is gearing up for increased numbers of visitors and pilgrims who have heard about this gem of a place, and in particular its striking basilica-style church. Dedicated in 2000 but still being decorated with an ambitious and fierce commitment to artistic excellence, the Church of the Transfiguration is where Community members gather daily for Eucharist and to chant the psalms in Latin. (Most days, the Divine Office is said four times, condensed from the traditional schedule of seven or eight times daily.)

Before ground was even broken for this church in the 1990s, a planning committee met for five years and decided that the building needed to express three fundamental aspects of the Community's character. It needed to be ecumenical, so the committee eventually rejected a considered Gothic design in favor of the simple Roman architecture that is the basilica style. This was not so much for aesthetic reasons as theological and historical ones: The basilica style predates all of the ugly divisions within the Christian church, and is therefore ecumenical by nature. Second, the committee felt that the building should express the Community's increasingly important monastic identity. "One traditional image of the monastic life is as a lifelong pilgrimage," says Father Martin, an Episcopal priest and member of the church planning committee, "The longitudinal design of the church gives expression to this idea of making our way from this life to the next. Every time we enter the church and walk the processional pathway, we are reminded of the heavenly 'direction' of our lives." And finally, the church needed to house the liturgy, to be a place where the altar would be visually central and members could comfortably chant the Divine Office back and forth to each other across the main aisle.

To these ends, every element of the interior design has been planned, prayed over, and executed with painstaking theological precision. All of the artwork in the church, explains docent Blair Tingley, is designed to preach the gospel to the people whether a service is taking place or not. In other words, even if no sacrament is being observed and no word being preached, people will still be spiritually fed just by feasting their eyes on the sights around them. Blair notes that in the earliest days of Christianity, people lived in "a visual age" because so many of them were illiterate that it was necessary for the sacred stories to be preached in art as well as in sermons, so ordinary people could understand. Nowadays, we live in a culture where nine-tenths of the people can read and write, but ours is increasingly a "visual age" as well, simply because of the profound impact of modern visual media. Preaching the gospel through sight, as well as through the oral and written word, can reach many people today who might not otherwise be stirred by its message.

Pilgrims who come here on retreat often spend much of their time in the church, partaking of the Community's worship life and chanting the psalms. They could not hope for a more appropriate site for transformation, since the entire church is constructed around the foundational theme of transfiguration. To teach the gospel from start to finish, the building presents the salvation history of humankind, from Genesis to Revelation. The storytelling begins even before visitors step inside the church. The outer doors depict Adam and Eve in the Garden of Eden (with foliage conveniently covering their newfound nakedness), while the lintel above the doors is an abstract representation of God's creating the world from formlessness and void. After visitors enter the church—usually by a smaller side door, since the front doors weigh approximately 4,000 pounds and are used only on Sundays and for special church occasions—the theme of salvation history continues as the marble floor mosaic depicts the murderous tale of Cain and Abel, showing why God's salvation was in fact necessary. The floor mosaic, with its two million pieces of hand-cut marble, then surrounds the baptismal font with images of the Great Flood before continuing up the main aisle and finally bursting into a Tree of Life at the altar. Careful eyes will observe that the roots of that Tree of Life can be found all the way at the back of the church, where they are symbolically nourished by the waters of the baptismal font.

The Bible's story of salvation history is told not just in the floor but also in the frescoed walls above, which depict twelve scenes from Jesus' birth, life, ministry, and passion. The mural sequence begins just to the left of the apse and wraps the entire nave in fresco—from front to back on the left side and then back to front on the right. These biblical scenes are interspersed with frescoes of modern-day pilgrims from every continent walking forward toward the rounded apse at the front of the church, with its enormous mosaic of Jesus, arms outstretched to receive them. When completed, these murals will be a visual demonstration of Christianity's most cherished hope: that all nations and peoples will someday come to Christ.

Just below the large frescoes are "spandrels," small triangular frescoes that depict Old Testament scenes relevant to the more imposing New Testament scenes above. Thus, the expansive rectangular fresco depicting the feeding of the multitude (where Jesus miraculously provided for thousands of people from five loaves and two fish) is accompanied on either side by two smaller frescoes, one showing Elisha feeding the one hundred and the other portraying the indebted widow whose vessels were inexplicably filled with oil. All three frescoes express the biblical theme of God's miraculous provision for his people, symbolizing both the Eucharistic feast and the heavenly banquet to come.

But it doesn't end there. The carved stone capitals located just below the spandrels carry the theme still further, depicting objects and symbols found in the stories above. The two capitals that support these frescoes about miraculous feedings, for example, also address food and drink. One is about bread and wine, and the other about fish—cod, to be exact, a nod to the local abundance of that particular species on the Cape. Miracles of multiplication, the stone capital seems to be saying, are not restricted to long-ago events in Galilee: God is a miracle worker right here and right now. The artwork of the church beautifully articulates what every spiritual pilgrim hopes is true: that healing is available, that miracles persist, and that God cares about the least among us.

The crowning glory of the Church of the Transfiguration is the stunning front image of Jesus reigning in glory, visible from all angles of the church and unforgettably arresting. Whereas the floors are done in marble mosaic, the apse gleams with 2.5 million pieces of colored glass, some of it metallic. The effect is dazzling, especially at certain times of day as the sun enters the windows and catches the more than two hundred colors that comprise the mosaic, including the glints of gold that are scattered through Jesus' white robe.

Visitors are often startled to discover that some of the work on the mosaics, frescoes, and other art was accomplished by Community members, who hired master designers and craftspeople from Europe to plan and supervise the church's decoration but did some of the labor and installation themselves. "That's . . . that's just not *normal*," sputters one woman taking the church tour. "That's beyond normal." And of course, she's right: How many comparably sized Christian congregations undertake to not only build their own church, but invest it with world-class artwork? Blair Tingley responds that the Community drew upon "a real conviction and a sense of calling" in creating the church, "giving very sacrificially" in terms of time and money.

Community members didn't just help with the artistic labor in order to save money in the church's construction; the reasons were spiritual as much as practical. Part of its identity has become wrapped up in its powerful commitment to preserving and handing down the great artistic heritage of the Christian church. Some of those arts, like fresco, are in danger of disappearing altogether, while others, like mosaic, are still in use today, but mostly by the secular world: it's far more likely for a mosaicist to get a commission for an intricately tiled bathroom than a baptismal font. So to carry on these sacred traditions, the Community of Jesus has formed guilds where members become proficient at mosaic, calligraphy, sculpture, fresco, and needlework.

But it's not just the visual arts where the Community of Jesus excels. Another aspect of the Community's dedication to the arts is its recognition of the myriad ways that people experience God, and this means music, theater, and dance. Gloriæ Dei Cantores, the Community's internationally renowned choir, have toured throughout Europe and North America to critical raves, and its Spirit of America band is consistently ranked as one of the top community marching bands in the nation. There's a liturgical dance troupe, a chamber music group, a brass ensemble, a theater company, and a bell choir. Pilgrims who stay in Bethany House can catch music wafting on the air all day—the band practicing for its upcoming tour, a soprano going through her scales, a young child learning the recorder. It's no wonder that, when confronted with this tremendous outpouring of creativity, the visiting woman on the church tour labeled it "beyond normal."

At the Community of Jesus, where unfettered honesty is a spiritual discipline, such a torrent of creativity is the natural result of a life lived openly and in concert with others. Those who come on pilgrimage are privileged to glimpse in the lives of those who make their home here what lies in store further along the spiritual journey, after the soul has begun to make peace with God. This is a place of ongoing transformation, a spiritual ideal perhaps best expressed in the theme of transfiguration that characterizes the church of that name, the Community's locus of spiritual activity.

Gazing up at the church's oculus window with its theme of the Transfiguration of Christ, it's easy to believe that spiritual change is not only possible for those whose lives intersect with this special place, but inevitable.

FIVE

Psalms and Silence

The Abbey of Gethsemani
Trappist, Kentucky

In *The Seven Storey Mountain,* Thomas Merton's famous autobiographical account of his transformation from cosmopolitan bohemian student to Trappist monk, Merton writes wistfully of his first journey to The Abbey of Gethsemani in Kentucky. After getting off the train at Bardstown, he traveled by car the short remaining distance to the monastery, barely able to contain his excitement. Suddenly a steeple came into view from behind a rounded knoll. When the car crested the rise, Merton could glimpse the entire abbey complex framed by woods. The steeple, he wrote, "was as bright as platinum and the whole place was as quiet as midnight lost in the all-absorbing silence and solitude of the fields." Thomas Merton had found his home.

Nearly half a century later, Ohio newspaper editor Steve Pollick and a priest friend decided that for their first pilgrimage to Gethsemani, they would re-create Merton's own initial journey there, eschewing maps and using only the Trappist's physical descriptions of the landscape as their guide. Amazingly enough, they did not get lost, perhaps a testimony to the vivid detail that characterized Merton's writing. "It was kind of a trip of discovery for us," Pollick says of the 1987 journey. "When we rounded that last corner and could see the tower of the church, how excited we were!" Like Merton, Pollick felt the presence of God keenly at Gethsemani. "I've traveled all over the world, and I've been in wild solitude in the Arctic and the deserts, and I know God is everywhere. But I wasn't in those places particularly to pursue God. When you go on retreat, you're going there so you can pursue God in a new way," he explains.

At Gethsemani, little seems to have changed in the surrounding landscape since Merton's day. It's still a beautiful country, and wild. Indeed, it's not difficult to imagine what the area must have looked like two hundred years ago, when Abraham Lincoln was born in a log cabin just a few miles away. Although Bardstown is only a fifteen- or twenty-minute drive from the Abbey, there's a surprising remoteness to Gethsemani.

It is this very isolation that attracts most visitors, a silence that promises safety and peace. It is so unexpectedly soothing, such a balm to the soul, that after even a few hours of retreat, pilgrims may find the sudden jangle of the guestmaster's telephone jarring. Apparently, however, silence is not a favorite feature of Gethsemani for everyone. The monks say that a few guests have arrived for a week's retreat and stayed only a day or even a couple of hours, so distressed are they by the pervasive silence of the place. What most find liberating—freedom from small talk, empty chatter, the verbal clutter of life—others consider oppressive. And why shouldn't they? Silence is in every way countercultural. "We live in a society," wrote Merton, "whose whole policy is to excite every nerve in the human body and then keep it at the highest pitch of artificial tension, to strain every human desire to the limit and to create as many new desires and synthetic passions as possible, in order to cater to them with the products of our factories and printing presses and movie studios and all the rest." Given this feverish pace, it's no wonder that some pilgrims find the silence unnerving.

There are certainly places throughout the abbey where retreatants can enjoy conversation if they so choose: One of the dining rooms is set aside for talking, and it's permitted in some designated rooms and outdoor areas. But for the most part, silence prevails. One consequence is that unlike other retreat centers, Gethsemani offers guests a sort of default anonymity; they can choose to make friends and meet people by hanging out in the appointed conversation areas, but it's very possible to go for days without having to carry on a conversation with a single stranger.

The retreat house, built in 1952 and renovated in the late 1980s, has thirty-one rooms, each with a private bath. Rooms are simply but comfortably furnished, mostly with twin beds. Wall-to-wall carpeting helps to preserve the atmosphere of silence. The house is open to women the first and third weeks of the month, and to men the second and fourth weeks. There are also an additional fifteen rooms in the cloistered area that are always reserved for men. So at any one time, there may be forty-five or so pilgrims at the Abbey, some for "mid-week" retreats (Monday lunch to Friday breakfast) and others for weekends (Friday lunch to Monday breakfast). This means that in a given year, up to five thousand pilgrims might come and go at Gethsemani, though a former guestmaster estimates that the number is closer to forty-five hundred, since some people choose longer stays. Slots fill up rapidly; on the first business day of each month, the switchboard will be flooded with calls for reservations four months hence. The monks start taking January reservations in early September, for example. There is also a stand-by list in case of eleventh-hour cancellations.

The structure of the days at Gethsemani revolves always around the Divine Office, the ancient worship services that offer a sacred rhythm to ordinary time. As at other Benedictine monasteries, pilgrims are invited—but never required—to join in these services, most of which are brief. The sext (noonday) service, for example, is only about fifteen minutes long, with the monks chanting several psalms in gentle, rhythmic unison. Those who are accustomed to elaborately decorated Catholic houses of worship will discover that this church is unadorned, even stark; the walls are white-painted brick, and the high, narrow windows feature a simple geometric design. All this simplicity contributes to the peaceful, unhurried sensibility of the place.

In the church, a short glass wall separates the monks from the guests, who are welcome to participate in the chanting if they choose. Some pilgrims do so, lending their voices in song and bowing at rhythmic intervals during the office, while others simply soak up the experience and listen. At the end of compline, the last service of the day, a door in the glass wall is opened so everyone, monk and layperson alike, can file forward and receive a benediction of sprinkled holy water, usually from the abbot. All guests are invited for this blessing, though the Holy Eucharist that is offered in Mass each morning is intended only for communing Catholics.

For some retreatants, the monks' life of prayer is an example to follow long after the retreat is over. Judy Roberts, a freelance writer who has been making pilgrimages to Gethsemani since 1992, says many people wrongly imagine that the monks' lives are so wholly consumed with these daily offices that it's easy for them to find time for prayer. Rather, she says, the monks' lives are just as busy as laypeople's, if not more so, reflecting the Cistercian commitment to labor as well as prayer. They are required to support themselves financially, just like laypeople, an obligation that consumes much of the day. They manufacture and sell cheese, fudge, and fruitcake, and they run the retreat house. Like laypeople, they have to fix leaky toilets and pay bills and keep everyone fed. The difference is that they routinely stop their work at key intervals throughout the day to remember what is eternal, offering thanks for blessings and pleas for those in need. Such prayer is simply the rhythm of life here. Roberts, who sometimes struggles with insomnia, also says that she finds it intensely reassuring to know that if she is awake in the wee hours at home, the monks at Gethsemani are often awake too, holding vigil in a 3:15 AM service of prayer at Gethsemani. "It can be a very lonely feeling to be awake and alone in the middle of the night," she says. "It does comfort me that the monks are awake and praying at that time." Roberts also says that being at

Gethsemani makes her much more aware of all the useless noise that exists in daily life. "Everywhere I go, whether it's the doctor's office, or the grocery store, or the mall, there's noise. They even pipe the music outside!" she says. "When you go to Gethsemani, it's so evident that this is a place where they know how to do silence well."

Gethsemani is still a cloistered monastery, meaning that there is strict separation between pilgrims and most of the monks. A few of the brothers, such as the guestmaster, interface regularly with the public, and a chaplain makes himself available to guests for counseling. But pilgrims and other visitors are not allowed in the cloister, the factory where the monks make their products for sale, or the monks' refectory.

Also off-limits to most retreatants is Thomas Merton's hermitage out in the woods, because it is still being used for its original purpose; each week, a different brother gets the chance to use the hermitage for a personal retreat. For years, Merton (or Father Louis, as he was known here) had badgered his abbot to allow him to live as a hermit on the edges of Gethsemani, a plea that went unheeded until 1965, when the abbot finally relented. Merton spent his last years alone in a cinder-block hermitage on the property, cooking for himself and coming in only on Sundays for Mass with the brothers. Those final years here saw a remarkable flurry of literary activity until his untimely accidental death by electric shock in Bangkok in 1968, exactly twenty-seven years after he had officially entered the monastery. Although the hermitage is restricted, it is still very occasionally used for special visitors; writer Dianne Aprile, for example, who has spent some time there, called it "a thrilling experience." This hermitage stay was a pilgrimage-within-a-pilgrimage; she honored Merton's spiritual transformation even as she went about claiming her own.

For a Trappist monk, Merton's relative isolation was highly unusual. Ever a maverick, he was the first American Trappist monk to receive permission to live alone. The Trappist tradition, which is a reformist movement in the millennium-old Cistercian order, follows the Rule of St. Benedict's pragmatic blend of prayer and daily work, aiming for a communal and contemplative life. After its founding in 1848, Gethsemani had a century of slow and steady growth (with a few setbacks). But after World War II, in keeping with the rapid growth of postwar Catholicism, the monastic population at Gethsemani shot up to three hundred men; the Abbey was built for two hundred. Some monks were actually sleeping in pup tents on the quadrangle lawn. The abbot sent monks out into the world to found different daughter houses, all of which are still in operation today.

Gethsemani's monastic population has diminished somewhat, reflecting both the original decision to staff the daughter houses and the more recent national trend away from religious vocations. There are now around five dozen monks at Gethsemani, including a total of seven novices and postulants. Whereas in former years, these neophytes would have been young and relatively untried, most of today's monks have "been around the block," as guestmaster Father Anton puts it. One brother is a grandfather. The wisdom and settled sense that come with years contribute to the monastery's peaceful sensibility.

Some things about monastic life in Gethsemani are more relaxed than they were in the early days. In the nineteenth century, monks reportedly ate just one meal a day for most of the year, and the meal was soup at that. They slept on straw mattresses atop two planks, and flagellated themselves over the shoulders for any infractions of the Rule. Nowadays, the brothers sleep in simple but comfortable cells, and corporal punishment is a thing of the past, as it is for most orders. Other things have changed as well. Women were once forbidden from entering Gethsemani, where signs posted at the doors to the cloister cautioned that any who were found within the monks' enclosure would be excommunicated. But in the late 1980s, with the renovations to the retreat house, the Abbey responded to the many requests it had received and decided to begin receiving women pilgrims.

The practice of silence has also become more accommodating to circumstances. When Brother Frederic, the community's treasurer, first came to Gethsemani more than fifty years ago, the monks observed the practice of silence more strictly than they do today. "Back then, we weren't really allowed to talk," he explains. "We had a homemade sign language that we used to communicate. We could talk to the superiors occasionally. Gradually, all of that was changed. The most important thing about Christianity is charity, the love of your neighbor. When you can't talk, you can't console your brother when he's having a hard time." Silence is still important to Gethsemani's monks, who don't usually speak from 7:30 in the evening until 8 AM. This period is known as the "Great Silence" or the "Grand Silence," and is when each monk attends to his personal devotions, such as prayer, meditation, and sacred reading.

Although they are cloistered, the monks at Gethsemani remain active in the world and interested in it. On the morning of the 2004 presidential election, for example, NPR listeners all across the country were treated to an interview with Gethsemani's Brother Raphael, a World War II veteran who has lived at the Abbey for over half a century. He gently corrected the view that monks don't vote, and noted that they read newspapers and magazines, have Internet access, and are generally very well informed on current affairs. He also took issue with a reporter's question about monks "turning their backs on the world." Brother Raphael worries that this phrase implies that monks have washed their hands of the world, and "nothing could be more incorrect than that. My basic thing is to search for God, and to help others also reach that goal. I don't feel I've turned my back. I feel more deeply related to people in the world than I ever did before. I feel that much more so now than I did sitting in the lonely crowd at a ball game, where everyone is cheering but you have no idea who is sitting next to you."

Although many people have wrong ideas about what it means to be cloistered, the popular stereotype of monks devoting much of their time to prayer is clearly correct. The first monks arrived here on December 21, 1848, and Gethsemani's prayer tradition was set in motion the very next day: Since December 22 of that year, the brothers have been chanting the psalms seven times daily and having an eighth service for the Eucharist. They have not missed a day, praying their way through the Civil War, two world wars, a Spanish flu epidemic (which claimed the lives of seven monks), personal and monastic crises, and innumerable natural disasters. During this week's retreat a special prayer is offered for the victims of Hurricane Katrina, now raging; one of the monks grew up in battered New Orleans, and just received an e-mail update that his sister has had to evacuate the city.

Pilgrims who aren't accustomed to the chanting of the psalms are sometimes surprised by the sheer comprehensiveness of it. These aren't merely the praise psalms, or the psalms wishing for peace, or the psalms of Israel's triumph. The monks don't sing only happy praises but also the psalms of desperation and lament, including some of the passages from the oft-overlooked imprecatory psalms wishing devastation on enemies. But the monks see the imprecatory psalms, which are a legitimate part of the canon of Scripture, as honest acknowledgments of the reality of evil in the world—a recognition that occurs as early as Psalm 1, with its clear delineation of the path of the righteous and the path of the ungodly. "When we pray the curses, it's not about naming names or looking at a picture on a current 'most wanted' list," explains Father Anton. "It's about acknowledging evil and praying that good will triumph over it. Most evil is about one human being preying on another through selfishness. What we're praying for is for that cycle of selfishness and vengeance and hatred to end."

Every two weeks, the brothers intone their way through all 150 psalms, meaning that they chant the Psalter in its entirety twenty-six times a year. One brother who has been at Gethsemani for sixty-five years has prayed the psalms nearly seventeen hundred times, an astonishing figure to most modern people. Pilgrims sometimes ask the monks whether it gets boring, repeating the same words again and again in the course of a monastic vocation. The brothers say that, on the contrary, it is through repetition that real spiritual growth can occur. At different times in our lives, Father Anton says, the same words can mean different things. "Part of the secret of praying the Psalms is to put our story into the words. We're the people of God, and the Psalms are the prayer of the church." For pilgrims on a spiritual journey, the Psalms can become a significant catalyst for renewal.

While some pilgrims choose to join the monks in most or all of the daily services, others come rarely or not at all. Regular guest Steve Pollick says that many people are struck by the sheer freedom of retreats at Gethsemani. "Nobody cares, really, what you are going to do," he explains. "The monks give you a copy of the Psalms and their schedule, and they tell you what meals they're going to serve and where. But there's no policeman to tell you where to go and when." Pollick says that many people spend the first half of their retreat just resting and relaxing, and are "ready to listen" for God's voice after that much-needed period of stillness. The first half is a mere retreat, and the second half is a retreat of pilgrimage, the seeker listening with intent and the desire to be transformed.

Some hear God's voice most closely in nature. Eighteen hundred acres of the monastery are available to pilgrims for walking and hiking. Most visitors hike at least the half-hour or so that it takes to get to the Garden of Gethsemani, a sculpture garden in memory of a young Episcopal seminarian who died in the line of fire during the civil rights movement. The garden's centerpiece is a sculpture of Christ on his knees in desperation, his head thrown back and his face covered with his hands, elbows stretching like sharp incisors to heaven. This arresting image reflects an important truth about the come-as-you-are sensibility of the monastery, where many pilgrims have sought refuge because they are experiencing a crisis or some sort of crossroads in their lives. The Abbey's very name, taken from the evening of Christ's agony in the Garden of Gethsemane, offers comfort to those who are suffering.

In addition to the church services, the other major activity that establishes the rhythm of life here is the meal schedule. Food at Gethsemani is quite simple; guests file silently past a cafeteria-style buffet filled with mostly vegetarian fare. Lunch, which is the most substantial meal of the day, might consist of cheesy grits, baked beans, green beans, and some kind of soup. Breakfast typically offers hot and cold cereal, canned and fresh fruit, breads, and an assortment of cheeses made right at Gethsemani. Supper is typically light and may feature something that was also on the menu at lunch. At all times, guests can help themselves to hot and cold beverages, bread, and peanut butter, a helpful consideration for pilgrims who accidentally sleep through breakfast or want to pack a small lunch for day hiking.

Above all, Gethsemani is a sanctuary of peace and reflection, and any pilgrimage there offers ample opportunities to commune with God. As Father Anton encourages the retreatants, pilgrims can use this time to "just bask in silence." Freed from the pressing responsibilities of the day-to-day, they can delve into the deepest work of the soul. "Take your life," Father Anton advises, "and spread it out like a deck of cards."

Anyone Who Comes Here Is Just Who They Are

Mt. Calvary Retreat House and Monastery
Santa Barbara, California

The first thing you realize as you drive the twisty roads in the hills above Santa Barbara, California, in search of Mt. Calvary Retreat House and Monastery, is that this place lives up to its name—in particular the "Mt." part. You drive steadily up; your car engine begins to labor; you find yourself gripping the steering wheel more tightly to negotiate the blind curves that come one after another as the road hugs the mountainside. Then suddenly you come to a crossroads, literally, and realize you don't know which way to go.

Many pilgrimages involve a journey, typically a well-defined path that guides you to your destination. Though the way may not be easy, at least it's clear. Not so with Mt. Calvary. Signs pointing the way are scarce, and what signs there are, are small, an apparent afterthought. In fact, they seemed designed more to test your faith than supplement your sense of direction or the map you've downloaded from the monastery website. There is a small white sign at this crossroads that points vaguely left—or is that straight ahead? It sits at a strange angle, as if it once pointed definitely in one direction or another, but no more. Maybe a car hit it and knocked it out of alignment. Or was it placed carelessly? Or *purposefully*? (You have a momentary vision of two robed monks, one laughing in glee while the other carefully calculates the angle of maximum ambiguity and hammers the sign in the ground *just so*.) Your map is useless and both roads look as if they could feasibly lead up the mountain to the monastery. You can't call for help because your cell phone has no reception. Again, you look at the sign, more riddle than guide. You're on your own.

You choose a road, drive up it, and soon realize you've chosen wrong. You end up in one of the neighborhoods clustered at lower elevations, where the narrow streets curl around and twist back on themselves like fractal geometry. You try to get back to the intersection, but somehow only end up in a different neighborhood. Your pilgrimage has just begun and already you're lost.

As it turns out, getting lost like this seems to be virtually a rite of passage for first-time visitors to Mt. Calvary, who often swap stories about "coming up the mountain." They report being frustrated, angry, and impatient with themselves—some to the point (they claim) that they considered simply returning home.

Eventually, however, you calm down enough to reassess your situation, retrace your steps, and with a renewed patience get untangled from the houses and driveways and get on the correct stretch of road. You wind further up the mountainside until you come to Mt. Calvary's driveway (here, thankfully, is a large, unmistakable sign pointing you distinctly left). You turn in sharply, climb up the backside of a rise and come out upon it: the crest of a long, exposed ridge, an arm of the mountain open to the wide sky and reaching out toward the sea. At the furthest end of the ridge sits Mt. Calvary, perched there beautifully, overlooking the city of Santa Barbara and the Pacific Ocean. Now you take a deep breath; you've arrived. You once were lost, but now you have found your way. You don't know it yet, but this is a process you will find yourself repeating, in a spiritual manner of speaking, for the duration of your stay at Mt. Calvary.

For Mt. Calvary is a unique kind of pilgrimage destination. The monastery doesn't promise miracles, dramatic healings, or spiritual visions; the brothers don't promise to lead you to salvation, enlightenment, or even a life-changing experience. In fact, Mt. Calvary doesn't promise anything. It's not very dramatic that way. Rather, it's just there, ready to welcome you and whatever literal and emotional baggage you bring with you. As a result, the journey pilgrims take here is an interior one, often a trip into their own fears, frustrations, and pain—a landscape where it's easy to become disoriented and lost. You might wish for a guide with easy answers to lead you straight out of the confusion, but you're not likely to find that at Mt. Calvary. What you will find instead is silence, beauty, and support from others on their own journeys—and the realization that you are already "enough"; you yourself can face your challenges and find your way "up the mountain."

Mt. Calvary's front entrance is adorned with newly restored murals, and the oversized front door, all dark wood, is a heavy beast. You are greeted in the foyer, which doubles as part of Mt. Calvary's excellent bookstore, by one of the half-dozen or so brothers who live here, or by a member of the small guest-house staff. He has you sign in, shows you on a small map where your room is, informs you when the next meal will be (please arrive promptly), and gently encourages you to mind the Great Silence, the twelve or so hours of total quiet that begin at 8:30 PM and last through the end of breakfast the following day.

And then, much as when you faced the ambiguous sign coming up the mountain, you are guideless. You are on your own, left to discover your own unique path, your own particular way of being while staying at Mt. Calvary.

The guest house literature says it is "a ministry of Benedictine hospitality," and as you settle into your room, which is simple, comfortable, and clean, it begins to dawn on you that this is a type of hospitality you've never encountered before. A brother might ask with a mild grin, "Did you find us all right?" (And you wonder, "Are you the one who put up that sign?") But beyond the simplest greeting, no one peppers you with questions or get-to-know-you small talk. The labored, everyday pleasantries of *trying* to make someone feel welcome—"So, where are you from?" and "What brings you here?"—are supplanted with the simple reality that you *are* welcome. The monks' spirit of relaxed acceptance suffuses the place, and they allow that spirit to do its work in its own way and time; actual words spoken to that effect feel clumsy, redundant, pale.

A result of this stealth approach to hospitality is that Mt. Calvary is a quiet place. This silence affects people differently. Some worry that without the everyday props of e-mail, music, and TV to keep their identities intact, they will somehow become overwhelmed by the silence. One woman described how two of her friends who had planned on coming with her backed out at the last minute, because of the silence. "They were too afraid of what they were going to hear," she said. "They're more comfortable running through life because that's their norm, and the thought of quieting down freaked them out."

This reticence is understandable. Unlike other pilgrimages, there's nothing special to do at Mt. Calvary, no special site to see, nowhere special to go to culminate the pilgrimage experience. The brothers themselves simply go about their daily routine. It is very quiet. There is very little to distract you from *you*.

Yet for those who are willing to explore it, that silence can become a kind of companion throughout the rhythm of the day, providing a blessed opportunity to continually become disoriented to everyday mind-chatter and become re-oriented to the rhythms of the spirit. One retreatant named Evelyn described her preparations for her first trip to Mt. Calvary: "I thought the idea of extended silence was crazy. There was a mystery about it, like it's going to be weird, you know? Because it was unknown." But now, several annual visits later, she says, "It's so wonderful to be in such a tranquil and peaceful place. It's a gift to come and pause, to have the time to stop and reflect on what you're doing and why you're doing it. It slows me down." By taking the time to lose her everyday self of worries and concerns in the silence, she finds herself renewed and transformed. "It changes me," she said. "I carry this experience with me throughout the year."

But the silence is not aggressive. No one roams the halls of Mt. Calvary with a scolding stick to keep you properly solemn. In fact, Mt. Calvary can be noisy at times—most often with the sound of laughter echoing down the hallway or lively chatter over table at mealtimes. As you grow accustomed to the general quiet, however, you find your mental clutter is clearing away. You begin to remember, like discovering some elemental pattern you once knew but had come to forget, that silence is a natural and wholesome state of being. As you learn to cooperate more skillfully with the silence provided at Mt. Calvary, welcoming it instead of worrying about it, you begin to realize that it has remarkable transformative power.

Mt. Calvary is a ministry of the Order of the Holy Cross, an East Coast-based monastic order for men in the Episcopal church, and is one of five monasteries and guest houses the Order operates internationally (three in the U.S.; one in Canada; and one in South Africa). Although guests travel to Mt. Calvary from around the world, the bulk of visitors come from California. They come for the silence, and also for the unique ways that Mt. Calvary—and other retreatants—support and encourage them on their journey.

One young pastor named Ellen had four annual retreats at Mt. Calvary written into her contract with her church. "I find that pastoring can be more draining than filling, and I *have* to come here to restore my own spirit," she said. Over time, she has developed a set of personal rituals that demarcate her arrival and help her enter more fully into her time of retreat. "When I come I always do my opening ritual for myself in my room," she said. "I bring a bowl and fill it with water to remember my baptism. I light a candle, and I journal." As her quarterly retreat unfolds, she finds that she begins taking care of her whole self: "I hike in the canyon down there, and I read—and I sleep. I've been known to take a four-hour nap in the afternoon." What makes Mt. Calvary so conducive to this? "I feel held," she said. "This place is safe."

As it turns out, nap-taking is one of the most common activities at Mt. Calvary. This takes many people by surprise, as if they didn't know they still had the capacity to take a nap. Sometimes, over supper, the closet nap-taker will sit at table, stewing in guilt, and then burst out with his terrible secret. "I did it! I took a nap today!" he'll blurt, and the rest of the table will applaud—pilgrims supporting fellow pilgrims on the way, as they so often do—and affirm that it's permissible, even advisable, to give your body something as simple and fundamental as the rest it craves.

Another form of support for the pilgrim journey is the porousness of Mt. Calvary's schedule. This routine provides a predictable structure, but without pressure. One woman named Catherine noted, "There's something very anchoring about the schedule. Ring a bell, go to church, ring a bell, go to eat, ring a bell, go to church. At the basic level, your immediate physical and spiritual needs are attended to, so the stage is set for whatever else may happen in between those places."

The "church" she refers to are the five Divine Offices, prayer and worship services comprising a divine "work," or Opus Dei, as St. Benedict called it: Vigils at 6:15 AM; Lauds at 7:30; Eucharist at noon; Vespers at 5:30 PM; and Compline at 8:00. All guests are invited, but by no means required, to attend. Several minutes before each office, the bell in the central courtyard (which is also one of Mt. Calvary's wonderful gardens) calls the community to the chapel, a modern, white, airy space suffused with the smell of incense.

Like so much else at Mt. Calvary, the offices open with a rich silence. Then one of the brothers steps outside and rings another bell sharply to announce the beginning of worship. Depending on the season, day of week, and which office, the service could last just a few minutes or for close to an hour, with some combination of prayer, Scripture reading, and simple chanting. The chanting is compelling, not because the brothers are particularly gifted vocalists, but precisely because they're not; these are the voices of real men engaged in the real work of God, as polished or unpolished, skilled or unskilled as they may be—just like the rest of us. This, too, is a form of support for those on a spiritual journey, a reminder that you don't have to strive for something you don't already have. *You* are enough, already.

Indeed, anyone arriving at Mt. Calvary with romantic visions of angelic-voiced, austere, brown-robed monks subsisting on gruel and somehow subtly glowing with holiness will be disappointed. The monks are gentle, kind, and unmistakably spiritual, but you shouldn't be surprised to come upon one of them in the garden, enjoying a cigarette and talking about why he loved the latest Hollywood blockbuster. In fact, this "jeans-and-T-shirt approach," as a man who visits regularly described it, is part of the appeal and reinforces the idea that the spirituality pulsing through the life of Mt. Calvary is a powerful way of being in the everyday world. In short, you can take Mt. Calvary home with you. Besides that, it might not be a complete surprise that a monastery near the beach in California would have a more laid-back approach than you might expect to find elsewhere.

Just as many people go on pilgrimage with a general desire for spiritual inspiration or as a catalyst for change, others are driven by a more acute need. The same is true for visitors to Mt. Calvary, where it's not unusual to encounter someone working through a crisis or trauma in their lives. They, too, find support here. Jean, a mother who had recently been in a severe car accident with her young daughter, came to gain some perspective. In the ensuing months of shuttling her injured daughter to various doctor and therapist appointments, "it became clear to me how much my internal world has not moved out of that accident. I've just been in this reflexive, compulsive caretaking mode," she said. "I've been functional, but I haven't really been present." Mt. Calvary, she noted, is "a good place to come and get realigned." She even brought a photo album with pictures of the car accident and its aftermath, which she shared freely, unsolicited, with other guests. Sharing this story with others had a healing effect on her spirit.

Naturally, photos of a horrible car accident aren't the kind of thing most people would share at, say, a spa or on a cruise, but Mt. Calvary has a kind of easy gravitas to it; the people who come here plug into that spirit readily. They are, or become, willing to engage you in whatever state you happen to be in. Ellen, the young pastor, said, "People are interested and open and welcoming. It's good to be known, and here you can be known even if people don't know you. These are the kinds of people that I want to grow into being: whole, wholesome, holistic people."

Robin, who had come on retreat upon learning her father had terminal cancer, agrees. "Getting here provides me clarity. This place is so peaceful, it's a piece of heaven for me up here. And in how many other places do you walk up and introduce yourself to strangers? You'd never do that in a hotel. But here, it's just an instant welcoming and inclusiveness. And there's this warmth the brothers exude. This is their home that they're sharing with us, and that's part of sharing the love of Jesus."

She continued, comparing the world of Mt. Calvary to her home in Los Angeles. "The jadedness of L.A. is not even in this place. There, you're identified by what you do and what you drive. Here, it's about you as a person, not the 'you' you project to the world. Here, there's just an aura of 'We love you, no matter how screwed up your life is.' So no matter how jacked up your life is, this is a good, safe place to come." Or, as one of the brothers put it, "Anyone who comes here is just who they are."

That's how people connect at Mt. Calvary—happy or struggling, lost or found, simply as who they are, for pilgrimage is not a place for pretense. This is especially true at mealtimes. The monastery food, which is simple and excellent, is served buffet style from a long, low wooden table in the dining area. A large window at the end of the room offers a marvelous view of the mountains stretching along the California coast. Given the setting and the good food, people often find themselves engaged in genuine conversation about serious topics with someone they've just met, even long after the plates have been cleared. A hallmark of Mt. Calvary is the respect for the different points of view you'll find there. Ellen observed that "the conversations around those tables are fabulous. It happens every single time. And even if they don't believe exactly like I do, people are open to conversation. I've never met a defensive person up here."

Another beloved thing about Mt. Calvary that lends itself to a restorative, transformative frame of mind is its art collection. On every wall, on every horizontal flat surface, in every conceivable corner, is art. Paintings, statues, calligraphy, fabric, ceramics, trinkets; eclectic, you might call it, though certainly tasteful. Some of it is marvelous, such as the gold altar piece that dominates the hall outside the chapel, and some of it isn't. Taken all together, however, it adds up to a kind of gestalt of grace; at every turn, literally, there is a work of art to call your mind back to a certain vital way of viewing the world: through the lens of beauty. "Aesthetics are so important to our soul, and beauty—natural beauty and even the beauty we create—is so necessary for our being," said Ellen. "And here it's everywhere you look. Aesthetically, this is one of the most beautiful places in the world. Really. I soak it in through all of my senses. The architecture, the art, the furniture. Even the guest rooms. They're simple, but they're extremely comfortable, warm, and inviting."

Ellen always schedules her quarterly retreats for herself only, but not everybody arrives alone for private time. Mt. Calvary offers seminars on a variety of topics, such as understanding the language of religious icons. Some people come for those. Independent church groups often hold their own retreats here, and that helps explain why reserving a room at Mt. Calvary for a weekend can be so difficult; weekends are routinely booked up to two years in advance. Mt. Calvary also has a longstanding relationship with several twelve-step recovery groups, who often use the place for retreats. "Those fill up fast," said one brother.

The Order of the Holy Cross began holding retreats at Mt. Calvary in 1947. They were a hit right from the beginning, though things were different back then. "In those days, the retreats were conducted," explained a brother, "and they were only for men. Women were not allowed, except in a little chapel called the 'Women's Gallery.' In 1970, we started allowing women. Around 1985, we realized that the retreat movement was very big. We began to keep better records, and our ministry became also a business. And then groups began bringing their own leaders. See, in the old days," he continued, "everybody looked up to monks because 'the monks are the ones who know all about spiritual things,' so they would ask the monks to lead the retreats. And we will still do that if asked. But now, laypeople have more experience and understanding of the deep concepts of spirit and the heart."

Indeed. Just as many get lost on the drive up to Mt. Calvary but in the end find their way up the mountain, the monastery encourages retreatants to become lost plumbing these "deep concepts of spirit and heart"—trusting all along that they will find their own way to a new place of being. All Mt. Calvary has to do is provide the silence, the support, and an atmosphere conducive to the process. "When you come here, something happens to you," said another brother. "The presence of God in your life is more realized when you're in a silent place. After you've been around beauty, and you've been around something hospitable and loving, and you leave, you can't be the same. It may not happen immediately, but in the long run, you will remember this time."

PART III

✳

Crossing Boundaries

On a stone doorway inside the Church of the Holy Sepulchre in Jerusalem are dozens of small crosses carved by medieval European pilgrims, tokens of gratitude to God (a guide will tell you) for safe passage during a long and perilous journey across land and sea to this holy destination, the very spot of Christ's crucifixion.

Pilgrims have always needed to intentionally *cross over* into something new—the challenge seems to enlarge the soul and focus the pilgrim's intention. For pilgrims of old, the journey itself marked this crossing; the sheer physicalness and danger of the trip across geographic and political boundaries served notice to one's soul that this was no ordinary journey, but rather a pilgrimage with a dedicated, holy intention.

From this perspective, today's pilgrim generally lacks the benefit of hazardous travel. We can board a plane and fall asleep, both literally and figuratively. In our era of convenience, what challenge is there to wake the soul to the purpose of the trip? What keeps the spirit actively engaged with its holy destination? Are there new or different boundaries to be crossed—physical, mental, emotional, or spiritual—that serve as catalysts to make pilgrims *pilgrims*, not just *tourists*?

One such boundary modern pilgrims may cross is the dividing line between the secular and the sacred, as seen vividly every year in San Juan Capistrano, California. On or about March 19th, when the swallows make their annual return to the old Spanish mission there, the town throws a huge party. Yet in the very center of the swirling festival activity is a still point, an eye in the middle of the storm. It is a unique and compelling pilgrimage opportunity for those with the eyes to see it—for those souls able to leave the carnival madness behind and cross over, mentally as much as physically, into the realm of the silent and holy.

Another dividing line pilgrims may need to transcend is the one we create between each other's unique expressions of faith and spirituality. Who is "right"? Who is "wrong"? For many of the pilgrims drawn to Sedona, Arizona every year—millions of them, of every conceivable stripe and orientation—the spectacular natural beauty of the region helps to soothe the mind that demands such strict categories, and encourages instead feelings of expansiveness and peace. This relaxed and friendly state of mind allows pilgrims not to cross some perceived threshold from "wrong" to "right," but rather to discover a place that transcends such dichotomies altogether.

One begins to wonder: Just as the challenges of traveling across the literal landscape have largely disappeared, what will happen to pilgrimage when these boundaries of the interior landscape are too conveniently crossed? What new thresholds will pilgrims find to cross over then?

SEVEN

St. Peregrine, Pray for Us

Mission San Juan Capistrano
San Juan Capistrano, California

On March 19th in San Juan Capistrano, California, the preparations begin early in the morning. The "mission"—which today refers to a collection of buildings including a grade school, a modern church, and the 230-year-old remains of the *original* Spanish mission—is humming with activity. Late-running parents hustle their children, in costume for the day, out of cars and into classrooms. The kids reel and chatter with excitement, for this is the best kind of Friday: festivities instead of classes—a de facto vacation day. Beyond the school, among the tree-lined walkways, the sense of anticipation builds as people in clerical robes hurry down walkways and slip quickly through doors. The sun is not yet up, and the grounds of the mission are not yet crowded. Yet there's no mistaking it, it's in the air: *Something important is happening today.*

What's happening is this: the swallows are coming home, as they do every March 19th, to take up residence in their nests scattered throughout the mission, and the town is throwing a party to welcome them. Before the day is over, thousands of townspeople and tourists will crowd into the mission grounds to celebrate the swallows' homecoming. Most will be completely unaware that tucked away in the very heart of it all is a holy saint.

For deep within the mission—yet only a few feet from the center of the day's swallow-oriented activities—is a tiny sanctuary, an intimate shrine to St. Peregrine, a twelfth- and thirteenth-century Italian monk. Believed to have had an "instantaneous cure of terminal cancer" himself, St. Peregrine is now understood to have "powers against sickness of body and soul" in general and to intercede on behalf of cancer sufferers in particular. Pilgrims visit St. Peregrine's shrine year-round to pray for help and healing; the small room is worn, well-used, and well-loved. And on this celebration weekend, when the number of visitors to the mission increases exponentially, you might expect to find St. Peregrine's little room filled to overflowing with supplicants. But this isn't the case. Despite the throngs of people just yards away, only a handful of people find their way into St. Peregrine's shrine. Most remain outside, milling about the food stalls and trinket sellers unaware, or indifferent, that nearby is an opportunity to commune with something beyond themselves. Only those who through devotion or dire need transcend the festival energy of the day find themselves drawn into the little room to pray to the saint.

St. Peregrine's proximity to the madness of the party is a fitting symbol for the general condition of our lives. Many of us are easily distracted by frivolity or even the day-to-day energy of surviving, and we forget that very nearby—in the center of our lives, perhaps—there is the ability to reach out and commune with the divine. What is required of us is to see through our immediate circumstances and make a mental shift, come to silence, and experience the holy in the very midst of the everyday.

From the beginning, Mission San Juan Capistrano manifested the sacred-within-the-secular. The original Catholic mission at San Juan Capistrano was built in 1769 as part of the California "mission system," a system that by 1823 included twenty-one missions in a string up the coast as far north as San Francisco. This mission system was designed to bring Christianity to the native population, of course, but the missions were more than just religious institutions. They made wine; they taught construction and metalworking skills to the local population; they hosted rodeos; they garrisoned Spanish soldiers. They became the center of civic, economic, religious, and political life in the regions they served. Not incidentally, they also strengthened Spanish claims to the region then known as Alta California. In time the mission system was dismantled; mission lands passed into private hands, and mission buildings fell into decay.

In recent decades, however, there has been a renewed interest in these missions, and some have reclaimed an important role in the life of their community. In San Juan Capistrano, the mission complex is centrally located, both geographically (it's near a downtown shopping district) and emotionally (it lends the town a unique identity). But it's also a spiritual center. "Because this is a basilica," one resident said, referring to the modern church on the mission grounds, "it is encouraged in the Catholic faith that people come here to talk to God." And the attraction extends to other traditions as well, he said. "Everybody, not only Catholics, looks at this place as a place where you can come and be in tune with God and talk with him." His observation was borne out by the fervent devotion expressed by those pilgrims who made their way into St. Peregrine's chapel.

But on the morning of March 19th, the pilgrims are outnumbered by crowds who don't seem to be in a praying frame of mind. After some preliminary ceremonies, the party is kicked off with fanfare and media coverage in the grounds of the original Spanish mission, now partly restored. Two costumed bellringers wait patiently at the *campanario*, the bell wall, in which hang the mission's four bells. At the signal, they take up their ropes and with sharp, rhythmic tugs, ring the bells to call the swallows home.

Naturally, the bells aren't some kind of signal. They're not a starting gun. The swallows haven't been in a holding pattern just out of sight waiting for permission to enter the mission. Yet, you will be forgiven if, at the sound of the bells, you find yourself looking up, half-expecting to see a swallow flit by in search of its nest.

So just what are these swallows, anyway? Why this celebration in their honor? Not surprisingly, over time a body of stories and legends has grown up around the swallows and their return to the mission. As one early legend had it, the swallows that return to Mission San Juan Capistrano every year begin their annual pilgrimage—or reverse pilgrimage, you might call it—in the "holy city of Jerusalem." While crossing the ocean, according to this particular legend, each bird carried a stick in its beak. When the bird grew tired—*voilà!* A portable, floating perch on which to rest.

The reality of the swallows' journey is less fantastic, perhaps, but no less impressive. The swallows (cliff swallows, properly) winter in Argentina, migrating north beginning in February and arriving in Southern California—a journey of some 7,500 miles—on or about March 19th, which happens to correspond to St. Joseph's feast day in the calendar of the Catholic church. The main body of birds is preceded by scouts, which claim the best nests for their own mates. These bottle-shaped nests, painstakingly constructed from mud pellets, can last for generations and are often built under eaves or bridges.

This gives rise to another popular story explaining how the mission itself became associated with the birds, one that pilgrims and seekers of all species can appreciate. Father St. John O'Sullivan, head of the mission from 1910–1933, spotted a local shopkeeper knocking down the nests outside his shop with a broomstick. Father O'Sullivan, in fine Franciscan style, announced to the swallows that if they were not welcome in the town, why, they would be welcome at the mission. The very next morning, the story goes, Father O'Sullivan discovered the swallows building nests throughout the mission.

After the bells are rung at the *campanario* to ceremonially call the swallows to the mission, the action moves to the original mission's central courtyard, where a festival atmosphere prevails. Booths lining the walkways feature crafts for sale: jewelry, dreamcatchers, hand-woven baskets, handmade soap. Vendors sell food, from fry bread and *churros* to kettlecorn and pizza. In the old days, according to mission literature, this same courtyard was the locus of "colorful events and activities," including rodeos and fandangos, and the "townspeople sat on the roofs to watch young men demonstrate their talents as horsemen." Today's celebration is no less lively. In the middle of the courtyard sits a large stage. Throughout the morning, children from the grade school (also located in the mission complex) file onto it, class by class, each dressed in costume. One group appears in brown robes as monks; another as cute little multi-colored sparrows; another in the colorful dresses and sashes of old-timer Spanish settlers, their hair turned gray with that old theatre trick of brushing baby powder into it. As one class files offstage and another comes on, parents crowding the courtyard jockey for position and line-of-sight for their digital camcorders. As the day progresses, the entertainment will transition from schoolchildren to other acts, including a mariachi band, elaborately costumed Aztec dancers, a Native American storyteller, and a singer periodically offering earnest renditions of "When the Swallows Come Back to Capistrano"—the hit song written in 1939 that brought national attention to the little swallows and their journey to San Juan Capistrano.

It's easy to become absorbed in the energy of the entertainment on the stage, the offerings of crafts and food, and the general bustle-and-flow of a sunny, family-friendly festival day. But after a while, you begin to realize that you haven't seen any swallows. The little birds haven't made their triumphant entrance to the mission grounds, not yet. On other hand, "Mr. Swallow," a costumed, amusement park-style swallow mascot, has been highly visible, wandering the grounds, entertaining children and posing for photographs. Mr. Swallow, he's everywhere. But the real swallows are still a no-show.

You had presumed that people had come to witness the arrival of the swallows, like pilgrims expecting the arrival of a miracle. But slowly it begins to dawn on you that no one actually seems to even care about the birds, let alone *expect* them. No one pauses before the informative plaques placed here and there describing the swallows and their habits. No one ever looks up to the sky or wonders aloud where the swallows are.

But maybe the swallows themselves aren't so important after all; maybe the celebration itself is what really matters.

One man said, "Today is a family cornerstone," he said. "I see families I haven't seen in a year or two because they've moved away. So it's a homecoming for the swallows, but also for the children and for the parents." Others come for the sense of history in the mission. "I'm fascinated with the effort it took to build these missions," said one man who travels to several missions every year. "Tools were a lot more primitive. It took longer, and I appreciate that people made their own way back then." He took a moment to admire the buildings. "I *love* the history here," he added.

Yet, there are those few who come motivated by a spiritual need. They are the pilgrims, the ones who move through the carnival noise and bluster and enter a quieter realm. "Back in the church there," said one woman with her child in tow, "you can just feel all the different emotions, kind of like the past echoing, talking to you." She was referring to the mission's original church, called the Serra Chapel, a small sanctuary built in 1788. (It happens to be one of the oldest buildings in California.) And though the entrance to the Serra Chapel is just *feet* from the central courtyard and the throngs milling about there, only a few find their way inside.

This isn't a bad thing, for once you do find your way inside, the sanctuary feels like . . . well, a sanctuary from the commotion and noise outside. It's a long room, and a plaque will inform you that the walls, made of brown adobe, are four feet thick. It's also a narrow space, the width limited by the shortness of ceiling beams (that is, short trees) available at the time of construction. At the front of the sanctuary is a magnificent, 350-year-old baroque altar covered in gold leaf, brought from Spain in 1806. Paintings representing the Stations of the Cross date from the 1700s, and are also from Spain. A statue of St. John of Capistrano—the Italian saint for whom the mission is named—stands near the front. The entire room feels heavy, as if it were groaning under the weight of so many long years of devotion. "I feel the spirituality in there," continued the woman with her child, "the past, the present, and future all colliding in that one particular spot."

Yet among those who do find their way into the Serra Chapel, even fewer notice the small side door at the back of the room. This small unassuming entrance is labeled, simply, "St. Peregrine's Chapel."

Entering St. Peregrine's Chapel is like entering a womb. It's a tiny room, ventless, cave-like, easily twenty degrees warmer than the rest of the church. There are seats for maybe fifteen people. A bank of votive candles sits before a startling stone statue of St. Peregrine. It's slightly undersized; if St. Peregrine stood up, he'd be only as tall as a twelve-year-old boy, yet he has detailed, adult facial features.

He kneels, eyes closed in prayer or contemplation, a hand to his breast in a gesture of gentleness and devotion. His left leg has slipped out from under his stony robes; his knee and lower leg are exposed. He wears stone sandals.

If the energy of the celebration outside is missing in the Serra Chapel, it is even more solemn in here. The cramped space, the close air, and the iconography all help to slow you down. You begin to notice details, like how the red and blue glass votive candles flicker in counterpoint, or how the heat is laden with the oddly soothing smell of melting wax.

Those few who do enter come in reverence and with a clear purpose: to seek help from the saint. Unhurried, they come in a handful at a time. Often they sit in the chairs for a while, preparing themselves. Eventually they approach St. Peregrine, bring forth a votive candle they purchased in the gift shop, and light it. Then they kneel and pray. After a time, they rise, often searching pockets and purses for pencils, markers, ballpoint pens, or anything to write with. Then, without the least hesitation or embarrassment, they move to the edge of the space and scrawl their prayers directly onto the plaster walls of the chapel.

St. Peregrine's chapel walls are covered in these prayers. They are a kind of supplicating, holy graffiti. Most are direct and specific. "I pray for my friend's cancer." "Dear St. Peregrine, Pls make me strong to overcome my breast cancer." "St. Peregrine, please heal my uncle Russell though my family may not have religious faith, we have love and belief in god." Many prayers are in English; even more are in Spanish. *"Santo Peregrino, ora por nosotros"*—"Saint Peregrine, pray for us."

The party's outside, but the heart of Mission San Juan Capistrano beats in this tiny space. Most have come today for the celebration, but others have come—and some from a considerable distance—especially to visit St. Peregrine, diligently keeping vigil in his tiny chapel, a wound on his shin, offering solace and hope to those faithful enough to seek him out.

At first, you might miss it, his wounded shin. The artist carved a small gash into the saint's leg just below the knee to represent an open sore—the very source of the saint's cancer that, on the night before his leg was to be amputated, was miraculously cured.

But on the statue of St. Peregrine, the sore is not yet healed. It's a deep but delicate injury; the stone opens like a tiny blossom. And once you notice it, it's all you can see. It's a compelling detail, something remarkably familiar and human on a saint. It's a point of contact between the spiritual world and this one. Tomorrow this man may be healed and become a saint, but for tonight, he is suffering just like the rest of us.

One elderly man, after rocking back and forth before St. Peregrine in silent, intense prayer, tentatively approached the statue and carefully touched the wound—as if it were flesh, not stone, as if he were touching the flesh-and-blood sickness on his own son. In fact, Saint Peregrine's knee and leg are grimy from worshipers touching him there, reaching out to his most human part—his vulnerability, his weakness.

You presume that this elderly man has come asking for, maybe even expecting, a miracle. And a miracle may be forthcoming: Some of the graffiti-prayers on the walls record healings attributed to the work of St. Peregrine. One reads, "St. Peregrine, thank you for answering my prayer. Heal all cancer patients and take care of the survivors." Others simply thank him for a "full recovery."

Yet, the prayers written asking for help outnumber those giving thanks. Slowly it begins to dawn on you that maybe receiving a miracle isn't the most important thing after all; maybe the very act of seeking out St. Peregrine and finding your connection to the holy—whatever the distractions or obstacles—is what really matters.

It's difficult to leave St. Peregrine's Chapel. The residue of devotion acts like a little extra gravity, holding you in place for just a bit longer. But when you do step back out into the fray of the central courtyard, you find yourself momentarily disoriented. You wonder, "How can so much frivolity exist just *yards* from such a spiritual, intensely emotional room? Why do so few transcend the noise and distraction to find the holiness that was always so close at hand?"

Reflecting on both the Serra Chapel and St. Peregrine's Chapel, one man said, "Going in there is a unique experience—you feel a lot closer to *yourself* in there. Everything is all old and it brings to mind thoughts of how many people have been in there and all the things they've asked for and prayed for and thanked for. It's a healing experience." His wife agreed. "It takes you to another land," she said.

The celebration has lasted all day, and you have yet to see a single sparrow. As you begin the walk toward the exit, you come across a table tucked inconspicuously into an arcade behind some columns, offering literature and information about the swallows. You strike up a conversation with the woman behind the table who cheerfully informs you that the swallows no longer return to the mission at all.

This, then, is the big surprise: You never will see a swallow at the mission. As it turns out, in 1997 the mission buildings underwent earthquake retrofitting, a process that required the removal of the swallows' nests. When the swallow scouts arrived the following spring, they discovered their nests gone, and so guided the flock to a new nesting area, a community college a few miles away. With a smile, the woman behind the table provides you with a convenient map, guiding you to where you *can* see the swallows.

This news is disappointing at first, then you feel outright deceived. Then you wonder, Does it matter? The swallows were just the maguffin anyway—the excuse for a party, a reunion of families and friends. The real power of the swallows is not the swallows themselves, but the coming-together of the community to celebrate them.

So it is with pilgrims to St. Peregrine. Their prayed-for miracles may, like the sparrows, never show up. But this does not detract from the encounter the pilgrims have already had: the sure and tangible presence of the holy in St. Peregrine's little shrine, right there in the heart of the festival and, simultaneously, a world away. Blessed are they whose hearts allow them to step from the crowd, embrace silence, and cross over into that other realm that was always so near at hand.

Well, maybe it's not entirely our doing; maybe the saint has something to do with it, too. At the end of the day, one woman reflected on the saint's influence, whether or not her prayer was answered directly. "Every saint strengthens our faith," she said. "They're our brothers and they're constantly praying for us, so if we honor them, they give us graces. Every time I visit, I ask him to place healing hands about me and bless me, because we need all the help we can get."

EIGHT

The Mountains are Singing

Beauty and Devotion among the Red Rocks
Sedona, Arizona

Hundreds of millions of years ago, central Arizona was wet. Shallow seas and river deltas, flood plains and coastal sand dunes variously marked the landscape. Sediment and sand accumulated, was buried under more sediment and sand, and over time hardened into limestone, sandstone, and other types of rock. Fast-forward to just a few million years ago when tremendous geologic forces activated faults and other weaknesses in those rocks. Eventually, through the steady work of wind and water, these weaknesses eroded into canyons and valleys, leaving behind uneroded, often massive, stratified red rock formations in what by then had become a desert land.

Today, as travelers drive the road south from Flagstaff toward Sedona, they descend some 2,500 feet into one such eroded canyon—Oak Creek Canyon, lush with trees—and down through successively older layers of the rock; as you drive down to Sedona, you simultaneously drive backward through eons of geologic time. When the road reaches the canyon's mouth, the trees suddenly stop, and the view opens to a dramatic desert panorama: fantastically high buttes, spires, and mesas, each composed of distinct horizontal strata, like layers of a cake, ranging from sandy-light to fiery orange to burnt ochre to rich, deep shades of brown-orange-red that defy description. In one glance, these strata, the telltale sign of sedimentary rock, bear witness to tens of millions of years of blowing sand dunes, lost rivers, and disappeared seas.

Come to Sedona, and the beauty of these desert silent rocks will astonish you.

Deserts have long been conducive to spiritual experiences. Perhaps it's the starkness, which stills our minds and enables us to behold the holy all about us. Maybe it's the dryness, which creates thirst and reminds us that we are not physically, or spiritually, self-sufficient after all. Or perhaps it's just the sheer magnitude of the dry bare earth from horizon to horizon, speaking clearly of the trajectory of our lives: From dust we come and to dust we will return.

Whatever the reason, the desert landscape in and around Sedona is sublime, as travelers and pilgrims have been discovering for more than a century. Today, some four million people visit "red rock country" annually, of which (according to a Northern Arizona University study) almost two-thirds are seeking a spiritual experience. They come to Sedona for peace, solace, revelation, transformation. They are pilgrims in the wilderness.

Yet Sedona is a fascinating and uniquely American pilgrimage destination because it does not appeal to pilgrims of one faith only. Go up into the red rocks and you will find fundamentalists and skeptics, seekers and self-proclaimed heretics, each seeking to encounter the holy according to his or her understanding. Some discover it in and near the rocks themselves. Others find inspiration in an Easter sunrise worship service at a mesa-top shrine dedicated to interreligious cooperation. Still others find it by lighting candles and praying in the Chapel of the Holy Cross, a Catholic sanctuary built strikingly on a promontory as if the finger of God had drawn it up from the very rocks themselves.

But whatever their differences, these pilgrims are united in their common experience of the sheer beauty of the Sedona landscape. They may describe the experience differently, but they all agree on one thing: The magnificent vistas and rugged red rocks aren't just an opportunity for a pretty picture. The beauty here is something you *encounter*; it's a power that invites you, whatever your faith, to slow down and alter your established patterns of thinking and acting in the world. The experience of beauty may be subjective, but one thing is certain: In Sedona, at least, the beauty can change your perspective entirely.

To most people, Sedona is most closely associated with believers in New Age spirituality. One such believer, a young man named Peter, took a year off between high school and college to make a pilgrimage to Sedona. He journeyed from Massachusetts with a friend to experience the beauty of the rocks, where he and his friend hung out, illegally hawking crystals and handmade trinkets to tourists taking in the view. ("Like, if we get caught selling this stuff, it's a five hundred dollar fine," he said.) At night, they unfurled their sleeping bags and slept out under the stars. One evening as he closed up his crystal "shop," Peter pointed out across the valley and said, "See those red rocks over there? Looking at that big red rock formation *does something* to you. It's stimulating without being jarring or tense. It heightens your awareness."

When we journey forth on pilgrimage, we expect to encounter something new. We open our senses and become more willing to experience the unknown or the unusual; we have a heightened willingness to touch—and be touched by—the spiritual. In colorful language Peter, in describing the effect of the rocks across the valley, was describing what forest-dwellers and desert-wanderers of many faiths have recognized from the beginning: that we are not separate from creation; that the outer, physical landscape can help us chart the inner, spiritual one; that the land itself harbors a unique power to awaken and inspire our souls.

And Peter was right. The various shades of brown and red in the rocks across the valley seemed to be fluid; their colors had become richer and more nuanced with the fading daylight and deepening of blue evening skies. Through a trick of perspective, or of the limitations of the human eye, or the influence of some kind of strange energy, the rocks across the valley seemed to be distant and, simultaneously, close. You felt that if you extended your arm, somehow your fingers would reach all the way over there and touch the lovely rocks, still warm from sunshine. This had a calming effect; you felt somehow less like an observer looking at mountains, and more like you, too, were a part of the landscape. Beholding the rocks altered your perspective.

Peter had an elaborate and surprisingly eloquent system of belief built up around experiences such as this of Sedona. "Rocks, animals, people—we're all just bodies of energy, resonating at different frequencies. So those mountains over there aren't just big piles of rock with trees on top—they're emanating a lot of energy that's vibrating just under the surface, at different frequencies. One way of putting it is, 'The mountains are singing.'"

Peter had also come to explore the vortexes famously associated with Sedona. These vortexes (locals seem to prefer "vortexes" over "vortices") are some half-dozen nodes of spiritual energy that became popularized in the 1980s. Just as the origins of older, more traditional pilgrimage sites are sometimes attested to only by sketchy tales and dubious legends, precisely how Sedona's vortexes came to be recognized—or even how many there are or what exactly they do—is hard to pin down. Walk into almost any shop or convenience store in town and you'll find books and pamphlets galore on the topic, often differing on the details. Some even weave elaborate cosmologies with regard to these vortexes. Others state more simply that "a vortex is a place in nature where the Earth is exceptionally healthy" and that "the energy of a vortex acts as an amplifier. . . . The energy will amplify—or magnify—what we bring to it, whether on a physical, mental, emotional, or spiritual level." What all theories agree on is that vortexes are places of concentrated positive energies that tend to encourage feelings of peace and positivity.

It might be easy to write off the idea of vortexes as so much hocus-pocus, but it's true that while you're in Sedona, you are likely to find yourself (perhaps even despite your expectations) feeling lighter somehow, less burdened, friendlier. And, if nothing else, the concept of vortexes provides a handy if somewhat mysterious explanation for the very real experience of heightened spiritual power in a particular location—a convenient way for the pilgrim to remember, describe, and convey the *mystery* of the experience itself. Using an unlikely image to describe a spiritual reality is an ancient impulse: "vortexes" mark nodes of spiritual energy in Sedona the same way, perhaps, that a "burning bush" marked Moses' holy ground.

What's more, the idea of vortexes aren't the province of New Age believers alone—another mark of Americans' distinct willingness to absorb elements of diverse belief systems into their own. One man who identified himself as a devout Christian didn't see any conflict between the notion of vortexes and his own faith at all. "I was up there praying to Jesus," he said. "If there's a vortex, then it's part of the world that God created, so to me, it's a holy site. It's a holy site for everyone."

The vortexes are not the only sacred sites around Sedona. Not far from downtown Sedona is Airport Mesa, so called because it's so flat there is, in fact, an airport on top of it.

Also on top of Airport Mesa is the Shrine of the Red Rocks, constructed in 1961 as a "monument to cooperation and religious beliefs." Although the shrine itself consists of little more than a platform and a large cross, its elevated position offers commanding views across the wide valley to some of the area's most dramatic red rock formations, including Capitol Butte and Coffee Pot Rock (which does indeed look like an old percolator-style coffee pot).

Daniel and Susan, a couple from New Mexico, drove to the top of Airport Mesa long before dawn to attend an annual Easter Sunday sunrise service, sponsored by several local evangelical Christian congregations, at the Shrine of the Red Rocks. They arrived extra early because they wanted to see the sun actually come up. They sat near the shrine in the dark, looking out over the valley, waiting for the light to rise.

At first, their conversation was dominated by sharply defined categories of religion and faith, and they seemed eager to contrast themselves against Sedona's New Age believers. "Sedona has a reputation for having so much New Age mystic-type stuff," said Daniel, emphasizing, "that's *not* what drew us here. We wanted to come and worship the Lord."

After a time, the sky began to lighten with a pre-dawn bluish-ness, and you could begin to make out Capitol Butte and Coffee Pot Rock across the valley, and the beauty of the land began to reveal itself. "Just look at this view," said Daniel. "This is so peaceful."

"This is a very special place," added Susan. She pointed at the rock formations across the valley, now beginning to glow warmly with the first direct sunlight of the day. "Look what the Lord has created. It's so pleasing."

Although their manner of describing it was different from Peter's, they were beginning to experience the same awe and wonder Peter felt while looking at his rocks. Indeed, as the light came up more brightly and the rocks across the valley seemed to take on a different personality every few minutes, something seemed to shift in Daniel and Susan. The thoughts they expressed became more porous. Their vocabulary of faith didn't change, but their way of speaking became more thoughtful, curious, and expansive; they started talking more about who and what they were, not about who or what they *weren't*. Their perspective changed. In a word or two, they relaxed.

In Sedona, the quality of light works a magic on the rocks according to the time of day. In the daytime heat, the rocks are bright and dry and seem to burn your eyes like the sun on the back of your neck, but in the cool of morning, the rocks themselves seem to soothe you.

And there in the morning light Daniel, who had begun his conversation with tight definitions and strict categories, began talking about something he couldn't quite describe, something that approached *mystery*. He described the first time he drove by another Sedona landmark, the Chapel of the Holy Cross. "Years ago when we came up here, we wanted to go up to that chapel because it's special. You're driving by and you see it up there in the hills . . . it draws you!" he marveled—as much at his own ability to experience the mystery of being drawn as the chapel's ability to draw him.

Susan referred again to the view. "Look at those mountains. Look at how beautiful," she said. She, too, seemed less sure of herself, yet more grounded and at ease. "Right now I feel the peacefulness and the beauty that God created for us. It's something deep down in your heart—it's one of those blessings he gives us. It's a joy to see it and be here."

Of course, while the region around Sedona is beautiful, so are many other landscapes in America. What sets Sedona apart? What makes the beauty here transformative, *spiritual*? Even those experiencing it struggle to explain the peculiar effect Sedona has on them.

Daniel and Susan couldn't quite capture it. Others attending the sunrise service were also stymied in adequately capturing Sedona's unique effect on their spirits. "It's just the surroundings, the glorious colors, the shadow and light-play off the rocks," said one woman. "And the wonderfully friendly people," she added.

"Clearly, this is inspirational," said another woman, sweeping her hand to the horizon. "There's a sense of inner peace. Beyond that, I'm not sure I can respond."

Peter had wondered if Sedona's effect on people wasn't at least partly a self-fulfilling prophecy. "People are completely unaware of the spiritual experiences they're having all the time," he conjectured. "But when they come here, they're looking for it. They'll come here and they'll say, 'I'm going to try to have a spiritual experience. I'm going to feel like God's talking to me, like Gaia's coming up through the ground.' And they say, 'Wow! I can feel something!' You know why? Because they're listening!"

He may be right, but many pilgrims come to Sedona with neither the enthusiasm of Peter nor the strict convictions of Daniel and Susan. They're seeking, but they're not certain what, if anything, they'll find. They come to the rocks with a deep curiosity and a genuine, perhaps unarticulated, spiritual yearning. These kinds of pilgrims may represent most of us—faithful but not certain of our beliefs; wanting to touch the holy more than we actually do; looking for a place that's familiar enough to keep us grounded but open enough to let us make that connection with the holy in our own way, in our own time. Many of these kinds of pilgrims gravitate toward the Chapel of the Holy Cross, built in 1956 a few miles outside of town.

From the beginning, the chapel was intended to inspire seekers of all, or no, spiritual convictions. "Though Catholic in faith," wrote Marguerite Staude, the chapel's designer, "as a work of art the chapel has a universal appeal. Its doors will ever be open to one and all, regardless of creed." She intended that the very architecture and artistry of the building would be "so charged with God, that it spurs man's spirit godward!"

Her vision was realized. The chapel is built directly on a red rock formation so that it appears to be almost an extension of the rocks themselves. Striking in its simplicity, compelling in its setting, the chapel looms above you at a precarious angle, as if it's shooting from the earth, like a diamond thrust up from the rocks. The spectacular red rock setting and the spirit of the chapel itself soothes you, slows you down, and encourages you to respond to the beauty all around you.

Tom, an American man, and Molly, his Irish girlfriend, came to Sedona because they'd heard so much about the area's beauty. They weren't religious, they said, but they found that Sedona, and the Chapel of the Holy Cross in particular, was an ideal setting to reconnect to the spirituality that was latent in them.

Molly, who expressed serious reservations about her own religious upbringing, nevertheless found herself inspired once inside the chapel. "As I was meditating there, I was able to block everything out. So I said, 'I'll just light a candle.' But then I hesitated, because I wondered if there's anything to it, you know? Is there any significance?" But she did light it, and said she felt "as though the prayer, the intention I lit it for, is being continued there until it burns out."

It's cool inside the chapel where Molly lit her candle. It's not a large space. Backless wooden pews wait for worshipers to sit and meditate or kneel and pray. The walls themselves are of simple, rough, large-pebbled concrete—the reddish hue recalling the dramatic red rocks looming just behind the chapel. A small altar is constructed of simple metal rods. Near the altar sits a sculpted face of Christ—"Anima Christi"—a kind of metal, modernist primitive mask, mildly unnerving with its smooth cheeks, closed eyes, unformed mouth—yet also somehow comforting in its simplicity and calm. The front of the chapel is composed of large windows looking out over the desert valley below. Integrated into the windows is an enormous concrete cross, which is not merely decoration, but—running from floor to ceiling and bisecting the window in three dimensions—is also an integral architectural component of the chapel.

A couple from Alberta, Canada, also encountered something spiritually compelling about the chapel and its setting, despite not being particularly interested in anything religious or spiritual. "We had no intentions to stop here," the man said. "We were just passing through. But then we saw the chapel, and *boom*! Even as I was walking up here, I said, 'I think that's a holy place. I can feel it.'"

They may have come to the chapel spontaneously as tourists, but their frame of mind changed. Instead of clicking a few photographs and leaving, they entered the chapel and lingered. Soon they found themselves beginning to dwell on grief and the recent loss of a friend. "We lit a candle and said a prayer for a friend who's a very big rock climber up in the Canadian Rockies," the wife explained. "A couple of months ago her fiancé was climbing, and he fell twenty meters and died. So I said a prayer for him, but more for her, the survivor, in the hopes that she'll find peace soon because she's really going through a traumatic time right now."

Contemplating death and grief isn't what this Canadian couple had in mind when they journeyed to Sedona. Yet beauty has a way about it—it can transition you with ease from rushing tourist to contemplative pilgrim. Whatever faith-language you might use to describe or understand its power, beauty helps you surrender distractions and timetables and instead explore with gentleness what's really going on in your own heart. Beauty invites you to expansiveness.

Indeed, natural beauty has the power to touch our spirits as do few other things. It can work a near-magic in its ability to slow our minds, change our perspective, and reconnect us to the sublime realization that we are a vital, but comparatively small, part of a very large creation. Our language struggles to express this; we resort to words like "splendor," "majesty," and "grandeur"—but such nouns only trivialize the direct experience of nature's song which, if you ignore words and go up into the red rock mountains near Sedona, you will be able to hear for yourself.

PART IV

✳

Modern "Saints"

Pilgrimage isn't always just about ourselves and God—just the two of us, enjoying a private and almost romantic communion. No, as Chaucer showed us so long ago, pilgrimage can sometimes be a public and communal experience, or even a rather bawdy experience. We hit the pilgrim road with others, often—but not always—people of a like mind and similar intent.

What's more, as we saw in the chapter on Saint Jude, sometimes we need intermediaries to help us to connect with the divine. For many people, especially those of a liturgical Christian background, the saints fulfill that purpose, interceding with God on our behalf and ushering the holy into the profane, everyday world. But for some of us, even the saints are a little too removed. It's a natural human instinct to gravitate toward people who seem to have progressed further along the spiritual path than we have ourselves. In this section, we look at two such great spiritual leaders, the evangelical Protestant revivalist Billy Graham and Vietnamese Zen master Thich Nhat Hanh. Since these two men are from utterly different religious and political backgrounds, at first glance they seem to have little in common except their ages: They are roughly contemporaries, with Hanh, born in 1926, being just eight years younger than Graham. However, as you will see from the chapters that follow, both leaders have acquired deep wisdom from their years of dedicated spiritual service, and this sagacity attracts many pilgrims who are seeking a more solid connection with the divine.

What's more, their itinerant ministries mean that pilgrims often don't need to journey great distances to see these sages in person: The sages come to them. Itinerancy lends a different feel to a pilgrimage to see Billy Graham or Thich Nhat Hanh. Unlike a traditional pilgrimage, the place itself is not important; a stadium or lecture hall or college quadrangle can become an ad hoc pilgrimage site for the spiritual traveler. Devoid of history, saintly relics, or holy architecture, the experience is stripped down to the pilgrim, the messenger, and the message itself. It's pilgrimage in its most essential form.

Billy Graham, yes. Thich Nhat Hanh, yes. But . . . *Elvis?*
Elvis seems the odd man out in this section of spiritual
heroes and exemplars, and in a sense that's true: He's of
course primarily and rightfully known as a musician, not a
religious figure. But the ways that many people relate to
Elvis, even three decades after his death, are profoundly
religious. This chapter on Elvis reminds us of two important
facts about pilgrimage: First, it's not just self-described
religious individuals who feel the call to go on pilgrimage.
As the long lines and weeping eyes at Graceland can attest,
pilgrimage is something that may well be hard-wired into
the human heart. And second, sometimes it's not spiritual
strength we're attracted to so much as vulnerability. Elvis is,
for many people, a secular saint who has been made perfect
in weakness.

A pilgrimage to Graceland is also a uniquely American
phenomenon. In our celebrity-worshiping culture, Elvis is
irresistible: He has the rags-to-riches success story, the stag-
gering charisma, *and* the tragic death, when any one of
those three would have been sure to keep his celebrity flame
alight for many decades. But there's something else about
Elvis, something that draws people in despite themselves. In
many ways a pilgrimage to Graceland reveals the underside
of the American dream as surely as its sunny potential triumph. Elvis's life becomes a cautionary tale of too much,

too soon, in a nation that has redefined the meaning of excess. As a pilgrimage experience, Graceland is a tribute to life's pleasures even while it serves as a sobering reminder of the fleeting nature of worldly things.

For different reasons, then, all three of the men discussed in this section can be classified as "modern saints." The first two are more traditional candidates for the label "saint" because they are widely recognized as virtuous and exemplary men. The third is a saint not because of the way he lived—anyone who comes to know Elvis's life will realize that his predilections for drugs and womanizing preclude him from the traditional moniker "saint"—but because of who he has become to the faithful in death. Though he was neither virtuous nor exemplary, his life continues to inspire millions, including the many who come to Graceland to pay their respects.

NINE

Finding Grace
in the Land

Elvis Presley as a Secular Saint
Memphis, Tennessee

"I think that Elvis will live forever," a fan declared to an online Elvis bulletin board community. "Not physically, that's impossible, but his spirit is very much alive today and always will be. I've never had the opportunity to go to Graceland, but I hope I will get there one day. Every time a song by Elvis is played, every time a movie with Elvis in it is seen, every time someone dresses up like Elvis, every time a picture of him is shown, he comes back alive again. That is what life is all about—Elvis."

It's difficult for non-fans to comprehend the single-minded attachment that such individuals have for Elvis Presley, that quintessentially American entertainer. And it's almost impossible for them to understand the pull of Graceland, the iconic Memphis estate he called home for twenty years and which now draws some 600,000 visitors annually. The opportunity to visit Graceland can transform even casual Elvis fans into spiritual pilgrims who seek what all pilgrims have desired since time immemorial: a sense of connection, a moment of transformation, and guidance on intensely personal matters. For such people, Graceland is Mecca, the alpha and omega of what it means to feel close to Elvis. The week of the twentieth anniversary of his death, a fan named Belinda reflected on her earlier 1995 visit to Graceland: "When I entered the doorway, all the years that I had wanted to be near him had come true!" she exclaimed. "I had been worried that going to Graceland was not the right thing to do, but as soon as I went inside I could tell that it was OK with Elvis to be there. I cried not out of sadness, but out of joy." Judy, another fan, says that it was her mother's lifelong dream to go to Graceland, but she died of cancer before that was possible. Judy says she "signed the wall for her," referring to an annual ritual that takes place during Elvis Week at Graceland each August, when fans can inscribe their names and messages to Elvis on an enormous wall. Judy feels comforted by this proxy ceremony, and knows that her mother is "up in the heavens with Elvis singing."

What is all this devotion about, this pious attachment to a brilliantly talented but heartbreakingly tragic figure?

Almost three decades after his death, Elvis Presley's popularity continues to grow. Half of the visitors who come to Graceland are under age thirty-five, so they have little or no personal memory of the man whose enthusiastic pelvic gyrations once shocked the American nation. Some visitors are here for the pure kitsch of it, to be sure—to chuckle at the shag carpeting and ogle the fleet of fancy cars that Elvis kept. But most come because there is an almost religious pull to Graceland and its former owner, whose spirit has never really left the building.

Entering Graceland is something of an affair. Visitors purchase their tickets across the street and catch shuttle buses to the mansion itself. By the time the famous music-staffed iron gates swing open to permit the bus into the curving drive, each tourist has been outfitted with a private audio tour headset, in which Elvis's voice is heard crooning a personal invitation via the song "Welcome to My World." The tour has no docents (though there are security guards posted throughout, should someone get too close to the "artifacts") and no common lecture, lending a private, intimate, air to the Graceland experience. Visitors file through at their own pace, and the headsets ensure that there is very little conversation. A respectful, almost worshipful, hush settles upon each group as visitors make their way into Elvis's celebrated residence.

Because Graceland is one of the most famous homes in America, and because Elvis is so connected in the popular imagination with excess, many visitors are surprised by the relatively modest size of the house. With eighteen rooms, it's downright small as celebrity mansions go. Elvis bought it in 1957 for just over $100,000, a sizeable sum for the time, but one the recently minted twenty-two-year-old millionaire could well afford. To Elvis and his parents, who moved into the mansion first while he was touring, the house must have seemed like a dream come true. It gave them privacy, which they increasingly needed as the publicity surrounding Elvis became invasive, and provided them enough room to offer hospitality to the members of Elvis's ever-growing entourage. But even beyond immediate practical needs, the house represented a seismic shift in the class expectations of the once-impoverished family. Gladys, Elvis's mother, had requested a home with a Colonial look, and we can only imagine that she gravitated toward the neo-Colonial architecture that was so popular in the 1920s and 30s because she had come of age in that era and probably never dared to dream that she could one day have what the other half seemed to take for granted. Graceland was a classy joint.

It's an elegantly built house that has, unfortunately, been frozen in the décor of the taste-free 1970s, fixed to the moment when Elvis died here. (The upstairs rooms, including the bathroom where his body was discovered, are not part of the tour, lending an even greater aura of mystique to Graceland and the circumstances of Elvis's death.) Some visitors chuckle at the overkill: the indoor waterfall in the Jungle Room; the white fur bed; the green shag carpeting that covers the stairwell walls—the *walls!*—leading to the basement. A basement den features televisions that run continuous 1970s clips from all three major networks, one of which features a shockingly young David Letterman.

But the ambience is more poignant than cheesy for most visitors, and those who are here for a pilgrimage experience rather than merely to satisfy idle curiosity will often discover something transcendent. Somewhere during the Graceland tour, there is always a moment of connection, when even the most Elvis-averse visitor finds something with which to build a tenuous relationship with the man. A Jewish woman notes how impressed she is with the donations Elvis made to charitable causes all over Memphis, including a check to the Jewish Community Center there; a self-professed bookworm is startled to discover that Elvis was a voracious reader who lugged a trunkful of books with him on tour and had a special reading chair constructed for the bedroom on his private plane. The Graceland tour offers these tantalizing glimpses into the person behind the kitsch.

Even the home's sybaritic extravagance endears Elvis to us, in the end. He is the Horatio Alger paragon, the hero who rose from obscurity in a two-room shotgun house in rural Mississippi to sell a billion records worldwide, more than any other recording artist. His meteoric rise cements our own belief in the mythology of the American dream. But ironically enough, that rise is mitigated in the public eye by Elvis's very excess. The fact that Elvis kept changing the décor of Graceland, hiring trendy designers and buying showy new furniture, reveals a man who was never quite comfortable with himself or his surroundings. It's a humanizing force, this over-the-top approach to money and to life. There's something sad but also boyishly appealing about a man who would just as soon buy a new acquaintance a lavish car as a donut, simply because he so desperately wants to be accepted.

The house is only the opening act of the Graceland experience; visitors can then file through various outbuildings that serve as ad hoc museums of Elvis's musical and film careers, family life, and automobile and plane collections. Throughout, the audio tour encourages a cunning familiarity between the visitor and Elvis, with inviting phrases such as, "It's not widely known by the public that . . ." or intimate details, like that his daughter Lisa Marie celebrated her ninth birthday in the conference room of the plane Elvis named after her. As they linger in that room, visitors experience a sense of immediacy, imagining that specific event taking place *right where they are now standing*. For Elvis fans, as for pilgrims to saints' sites at Assisi or Lourdes, such proximity is heady stuff, but even for more casual visitors, there is a sense of almost imminent contact with the legendary man.

The pinnacle of a pilgrimage to Graceland is the last part of the tour: Elvis's grave. And of course, this is the most humanizing element of all, not only because death is the universal leveler, but also because of the precise manner in which Elvis is laid to rest in the bosom of his family. Whereas other graves of prominent Americans stand aloof, both enormous and imposing, Elvis's is relatively unassuming, and is no more grand than the headstones of the family members who protectively envelop him: his parents, his grandmother, and his twin brother Jesse, who was stillborn.

Every August 16, the anniversary of Elvis's death, his grave is the site of a major processional, with thousands of fans filing past to pay tribute to their fallen hero. Most of these pilgrims are silent, with the reverent sensibility broken only by the sounds of soft weeping. But even on an ordinary day, Elvis's grave has the feeling of a saint's shrine, as the faithful leave behind objects of meaning for him and other visitors to peruse and mark. There is a bear from the Liverpool Football Club, and police badges from several towns in Massachusetts: Quincy, Braintree, Randolph. People leave flowers and angel statues, while some deposit photos of Elvis himself, inscribed with their personal messages to him. Cards, letters, stuffed animals, religious tracts: All these offerings testify to the enduring love of the faithful and their conviction that Elvis continues to bless their lives. One woman Denese confides to Elvis her wish that her mother could have joined her on this pilgrimage to Graceland to see where Elvis lived and spent so much of his time. Denese signs the letter next to a fuchsia lipstick kiss. Clearly, a pilgrimage to Graceland is simultaneously a public and a very private experience: These objects are here not just for Elvis but for fellow pilgrims to see and read. It strengthens pilgrims' faith to know that their love for Elvis, which they normally experience in a private and personal way, is shared by so many.

Making a pilgrimage to Graceland is but one aspect of the entire subculture of Elvis devotion. Since Elvis's death, fans have tended to regard his house, his clothing, his furniture, his very body as objects like holy relics that are worthy of preservation and veneration. (In fact, the reason that Elvis is interred here at Graceland in the first place is that grief-deranged fans broke into his first tomb in a Memphis cemetery. His father had his body re-interred here to protect it from grave robbers and relic-seekers.) Fans who were lucky enough to catch one of the items of clothing Elvis tossed out at a live concert regard those sweat-drenched handkerchiefs as ongoing vehicles of connection—with the man, with their younger and more carefree selves, and even with heaven, where they believe Elvis now, finally, resides in peace.

In the last decade, the Internet has become an indispensable place of exchange for Elvis fans, who swap stories of Graceland pilgrimages, post poetry about Elvis, and share anecdotes about how they once brushed shoulders with his associates or even the man himself. On Yahoo! Groups, there are hundreds of Elvis bulletin boards, some buying and selling memorabilia, others devoted to photos of the man, still others reviewing performances of Elvis impersonators. Elvis's reach is truly international; there is even an Iranian Elvis fan club with three dozen members. Like Graceland, the Internet offers a place where Elvis fans can share what is essentially a private devotional experience with other like-minded people.

In addition to the fan sites, Elvis has spawned several bona fide religions with their own rituals, holidays, membership criteria, and ministers. At the website of "Minister Anna" in Australia, we are reminded that Elvis has a hunka burnin' love for whosoever believeth in him. In her sermon, "You Are Nothing if Not a Hound Dog," Minister Anna encourages believers to come unto their King and love him tender, love him true. She wants them to not only indulge, but gorge themselves on pleasure; to live extravagantly and joyfully, celebrating Elvis's own approach to life. To that end, the site includes some of the obligations for church membership: for example, members must face Las Vegas daily, make a pilgrimage to Graceland at least once in their lives, and observe strict dietary laws. Every Presleyterian is required to keep thirty-one of Elvis's favorite foods constantly on hand, including banana pudding, which is to be made fresh every night. "Imagine if Elvis was on your *very street* and He passed over your house because you didn't have that banana pudding," explains "Dr. Edwards," the American founder and official theologian of the now-international denomination. "Or if you had it—but it wasn't fresh."

Obviously, this religion is meant to be regarded with tongue firmly in cheek. Its creation is simultaneously a loving spoof of organized religion and an insider's joke about how devoted some fans are to Elvis. On the other hand, all of the same impulses that characterize established, "real" religions are true of this church as well: People coalesce around a charismatic figure, establish guidelines for how best to revere that figure, and employ special rituals to mark important occasions, such as the anniversaries of Elvis's birth and death. As Erika Doss observes in *Elvis Culture:*

Fans, Faith, Image, Elvis religions like the Presleyterian Church have their prophets (Elvis impersonators), sacred texts (Elvis records), shrines (Elvis's birthplace and grave site), and place of pilgrimage (Graceland). The annual ritual of Elvis Week, which seems only to be growing in popularity, testifies to the strength of a religion in the making.

Naturally, not all Elvis fans belong to, or even are aware of, new religions like the Presleyterian church. But it's remarkable just how often fans use explicitly religious language to describe their love for Elvis and relationship to him. They may not be joining the Presleyterians in the light-hearted sacrament meal of peanut-butter-and-banana sandwiches, but many join in the general notion that Elvis retains an almost mystical presence on this earth. These are not the fans who claim, for various reasons, that Elvis didn't actually die and is simply in hiding to protect his privacy, the fans who note with knowing certainty that "Elvis" is merely an anagram for "lives." Rather, these are fans who acknowledge and mourn the reality of his death, but believe that he still looks out for them from beyond the veil. Dave, for example, claims that Elvis influenced him to keep going after being paralyzed from the neck down in a 1984 car accident. "I encountered him in a dream telling me to go on, pursue things that normally I wouldn't have taken the time for, uninjured," Dave says. "I awoke the next morning, encouraged, and have since then written a novel, movie script, and countless songs and poems. Generous to a fault, Elvis still reaches out helping others, through his music, inspiration, and tough path to the top." Dave doesn't contend that Elvis miraculously healed him of his injuries; Dave is still a quadriplegic and expects to be permanently paralyzed. But through this mystical dream of Elvis, Dave was inspired to realize that his life had not ended with the accident. Instead, he could push himself to try new things and tap into his creativity.

Why do such people invest a long-dead entertainer with the power to sustain and help the living? Why does Elvis continue to hold us in thrall? In the first place, of course, there's the simple fact that we live in a celebrity-obsessed culture that cannot get enough of actors, musicians, and entertainers of all stripes. These people don't even have to possess one iota of the raw talent Elvis displayed to inspire our fascination, so it's no wonder that we can't forget him. He's the North Star to which many musicians, from the Beatles to Bruce Springsteen, have compared themselves, and it's no exaggeration to say that he almost single-handedly altered the course of the nation's popular culture.

Then, too, there can be something innately private and close about the act of listening to music. When fans remember Elvis, they are also remembering, say, the times when their high school boyfriends cruelly broke up with them and they listened to a 45 of "Are You Lonesome Tonight?" over and over in the sanctuary of their childhood bedrooms. In other words, the voices of great musicians become interwoven with the hidden joys and pleasures of the whole round of life. Fans feel that Elvis was there with them through thick and thin, in all kinds of circumstances—the joy of first love, the senseless devastation of the Vietnam War—because they never stopped listening to his music during those times, and will always associate certain songs with those intensely personal moments. They love Elvis because he first loved them, through hell and back.

But the most important reason is that Elvis is, quite simply, the closest thing we have in America to a secular saint, who inspires devotion not for his miracles or holiness but because he could have used a miracle or two himself. Take away the purple Caddy and the excessive jungle décor of Graceland, and you have a man who is just like us. We can relate to Elvis, and so we protect him with an almost hysterical devotion and loyalty. And since he was such an unfocused spiritual pilgrim himself—his restlessness apparent in everything from his eclectic religious reading to his love for gospel music to his commitment to the martial arts—Elvis's home makes for an inherently sympathetic pilgrimage site. We feel that Elvis, of all people, would have understood why we are here. He himself was the consummate seeker.

At Graceland, the tour glosses over some of the most troubling aspects of Elvis's life: We see photos of him and Priscilla as a happy, loving couple, but there's no mention of the fact that she spent much of her adolescence under Elvis's roof and in his care, as he groomed her for a future wifely role. Their eventual divorce is mentioned only in passing, as are the drug addictions that eventually claimed his life. The tour, such as it is, is a gentle fiction, a healing portrait of Elvis the way we wish to remember him.

People don't come to Graceland for the Elvis who is all sweetness and light. Neither, however, do they wish to be explicitly reminded of his potent dark side. They already know this, and they are here because they love him regardless. A similar scenario has been occurring across the Atlantic. In 1997, Princess Diana and Mother Teresa died within days of each other. It's certainly true that Diana's death was tragic and unexpected, whereas Mother Teresa was old and had been ailing for some time. But do youth and sudden death alone explain the public outpouring of grief for the princess? In *Lifecraft*, Unitarian minister Forrest Church muses on this phenomenon, wondering why Diana should receive global media attention while one of the holiest persons of the modern era should pass away so quietly. But that, Church suddenly realizes, is precisely the point: We revere Mother Teresa, even love her, but we know we could never be like her. We will never be intimate with her. Diana, on the other hand, is a delightful screw-up as a saint, full of vanity, self-destructive tendencies, and broken relationships. We understand her viscerally. Church writes:

We admire other people's strength, but when it comes right down to it, their weakness strikes a closer chord. We don't identify with Princess Diana because she was royal, or because she was beautiful. We identify with her because we could see our tears in her eyes.

Diana is honored as a secular saint because she was a wounded healer, one who had love to spare for everyone save herself. Just like Elvis. Just like us. If it's frailty we're attracted to, like moths to a flame, we can embrace Elvis because he was so exposed, so unsure of himself, so *needy*. He and Diana were both achingly vulnerable and unable to hide their pain.

And so we come to Graceland, paying tribute to the man whose life was larger than life, and whose death places all deaths in sharp relief because of its grotesque senselessness. Although many of the people who make a pilgrimage to Graceland would not describe themselves as religious, paying homage to Elvis here is a profoundly religious act, demonstrating the human need for transcendent meaning in lives that are simultaneously ordinary and extraordinary. Perhaps it's no coincidence that Elvis was attracted to an estate that came ready-made with the name "Graceland." Like Elvis, the great but tragic figure we are here to honor, we come to this place seeking assurance that there is, in fact, still grace in the land—grace that can cover our diverse array of sins.

TEN

Just This

*Thich Nhat Hanh's Alms Round
and Dharma Talk
Fountain Valley, California*

O ne clear, bright morning, ruby-red banners were hung from trees in a municipal park in Fountain Valley, California. These weren't the kind of cheap vinyl advertising banners that you can stretch from tree to tree or from lamppost to lamppost. Rather, these were handcrafted fabric banners, dozens of them, simple rectangles slung from the branches and blowing casually in the breeze, like somebody's crazy-beautiful red laundry.

The banners had writing on them. In a lovely, semi-cursive script, some read, "Breathe, You Are Alive." Others said, "Misfortune Swept Away, Opportunities in Abundance" or "You have arrived, you are home." Still others read, "Today I Say, 'Today is a Day.'"

If you weren't familiar with Zen Buddhist monk, writer, and peace activist Thich Nhat Hanh or his teachings, such slogans could easily strike you as cryptic, inane, or as so much marketing huff-and-puff dreamt up by some flash-in-the-pan self-help guru. But for the hundreds of people who began collecting in the park awaiting the arrival of their beloved teacher, these aphorisms were familiar touchstones expressing profound truths.

But even if you'd never heard of Thich Nhat Hanh, even if you'd just been out walking your dog in the park early that weekend morning, coming upon the banners you would have paused and looked again. These written-on pieces of red fabric were utterly compelling in their simplicity, in the way they hung from the branches vibrant but serene, as if they *belonged* there, as if the trees had been speaking these messages all along in their gentle tree-language and finally someone listened, wrote them down, and put them on display for the rest of us to read. They just felt *true*, like a secret about the world you knew when you were a child.

Those of us who go on pilgrimage crave experience. We want to understand with our minds, believe with our hearts, and feel the pilgrimage experience with our bodies. Pilgrimage is a whole-person endeavor. Indeed, as Thich Nhat Hanh himself frequently affirms, the point of spiritual instruction is not to believe one teaching over another, but rather to lead you to a liberating *experience* of transformation. Once the transformation is gained, the teachings are used up, like a match that has done its job of starting a fire and is consumed in the process. For those gathered in the park in Fountain Valley eagerly awaiting Thich Nhat Hanh's arrival, the banners were the day's first invitation to not just hear a spiritual teaching but to move into the realm of experiencing the expansiveness of soul that these teachings describe and inspire.

Before long, Thich Nhat Hanh arrived, a slight man dressed in brown monk's robes, along with a thick brown overcoat and knit brown hat to protect against the morning chill. He walked down a path through the park, gently and unhurried—a deliberate, mindful walking meditation. Following him was a long, slowly moving line of some two hundred monks and nuns, also dressed in brown monastic attire. Watching the line move along was like watching a languorous river flowing.

This particular procession was known as an alms round, which is what it sounds like: The monks and nuns walked through the park with simple bowls to receive gifts of food and other necessities. They weren't out begging from strangers, however; this was a coordinated event. Lay followers of Thich Nhat Hanh had set up booths along the path near the red banners. As the monks and nuns passed by these booths, their begging bowls were filled to over-flowing with offerings of oranges, rice cakes, and other foods. Although this alms round was ritualized, it wasn't just for show. The nuns and monks were depending on these gifts of food for their lunch.

This procession also represented an unusual meeting of pilgrim and the object of the pilgrimage. Though you may have traveled to see Thich Nhat Hanh in person, the humble smile and gentle manner of the man as he accepted your offerings of food made you feel like *he* was the pilgrim come to receive blessings from *you*.

And in a sense, he was. This alms round was part of a months-long visit Thich Nhat Hanh was making to the United States from his home monastery, called Plum Village, in France. Plum Village has several satellite monasteries, including Green Mountain Dharma Center and Maple Forest Monastery, both in Vermont, and Deer Park Monastery, near San Diego, California. This particular visit was for a retreat held at Deer Park, along with other events, such as this alms round, a variety of public talks on partic-ular topics (such as transforming violence), and regular public dharma talks (discussions of key Buddhist concepts).

But while Thich Nhat Hanh journeys regularly to the United States to share his message in person, he is not a preacher or an evangelist for Buddhism, and he's not interested in converting anyone. In fact, he is fond of emphasizing the compatibility of different faiths, often drawing close parallels between the path of Buddhism and other paths, particularly Christianity. He is one of those teachers with a palpable *presence*; his openness, kindness, and soft-spokenness are deeply magnetic. Wherever Thich Nhat Hanh goes, people of many faiths show up, often traveling quite a distance just to experience the man and his message firsthand.

Michael had journeyed from Maine to spend time at Deer Park Monastery with Thich Nhat Hanh, whom he often called Thay (pronounced "tie"), a term of endearment. Over the years, he had explored a number of religious traditions and spiritual practices, including Christianity and yoga. But when he discovered Zen Buddhism, Michael said, "I realized that I had found my path. I had come home, so to speak." For Michael, Thich Nhat Hanh's articulation of Buddhist teachings is especially compelling. "I consider Thay a teacher of mine," he said, adding that he now makes it a point to spend time with him every year, however far he has to journey. These pilgrimages and times of retreat are powerful, he said, because they're a time and place where "all of us can come and whatever's going on in our lives, whatever's going on in our minds, the problems, the pitfalls, the neuroses—they're all accepted."

Finding acceptance and support in the community of fellow travelers on a pilgrimage journey is itself a compelling reason to set forth on one. The journey allows us to temporarily suspend everyday responsibilities that can distract us from addressing our fundamental issues and problems; the safe and supportive environment encourages us to bring our deep fears, worries, and everything else we keep stuffed down in our souls into the open and begin dealing with them. When our essential selves are laid bare, distractions fall away and we have the opportunity to reconnect to the world in a new, more direct, and more spiritual way.

By spending time with Thich Nhat Hanh, Michael often experiences just such a transformation. He calls it "groundedness"—"a sense of balance, contentment, and joy regardless of external circumstances," a mental space "where there's no discursive thinking, just the pure experience of the present moment. It's *just this*," Michael said.

Paradoxically, as Thich Nhat Hanh is keen on having you realize, this ability to focus closely on *just this* has the power to split the world wide open and move your soul beyond its self-imposed limits into a place of expansiveness and peace.

After the last of the monks and nuns had filed by the alms-round booths and received the offerings of food, they assembled in a tent set up in the park. Those who had set up the booths and other pilgrims who had come to seek wisdom from this diminutive Vietnamese monk gathered outside the tent. (Three sides of the tent had the flaps rolled up so everyone could see.) Thich Nhat Hanh sat on a slightly elevated platform and faced the audience.

After everyone was settled on cushions, relaxed on blankets spread on the grass, or sitting in their folding captain's chairs, Thich Nhat Hanh smiled and addressed the crowd by immediately emphasizing that this was going to be a time of both teaching and experience. He began with teaching, saying, "I would now like to give you some instructions on how to enjoy walking."

He was talking about mindful walking—the manner in which he had entered the park that morning. His instructions included telling everyone that, when practicing mindful walking, they should breathe in for two steps, then breathe out for two steps. As they walked, they should repeat to themselves, "I have arrived; I am home. I have arrived; I am home," always in rhythm with their breathing and their walking. "These are not statements to make," he said regarding the walking mantra he was suggesting. "This is a practice to realize." To prove it, he got up from his seat and invited everyone to join him in experiencing a mindful walk through the park.

Pilgrimages, especially more traditional ones, often involve walking to the holy site, not walking once you get there. But this invitation into actual experience was compelling, and remarkably hard to do. Until you try to walk slowly and deliberately, you don't realize how quickly you normally move through the world. This was a hallmark of Thich Nhat Hanh's teaching, and what Michael meant by experiencing *just this*: slowing down. Paying attention to this present moment, not what happened yesterday or even ten minutes ago, and not what will happen ten minutes from now or tomorrow. Right now. This step. Just this.

"Life is only available in the present moment," Thich Nhat Hanh said. "Let each step be solid and joyful. Walk like you walk in the kingdom of God" he said, calling upon Christian imagery, which he liked to do from time to time to emphasize the universal availability of these experiences. "Walk like you walk in the Pure Land of the Buddha."

This practice of mindful walking and breathing, while challenging, can be transformative. Howard was a pilgrim who had come to hear Thich Nhat Hanh teach because, he said, "I'm at a pass personally where I have conflict in my job and conflict *within*. This is a very peaceful and open environment, and it's all about mindfulness, mindfulness, mindfulness. They say, 'Breathe in—I am at peace. Breath out—this is a perfect moment.' It's not an easy practice, but it helps you quiet all these little voices going on in your mind all the time—they call it 'quieting the monkeys.'" By focusing his mind on the present moment, Howard said, "I've been able to quiet my mind today."

Even lunchtime was an opportunity for both teaching and experience; Thich Nhat Hanh had a way of weaving lessons into the most mundane moments. As people got out the food they had brought with them (or had been offered, in the case of the monks and nuns), he said, "A flower is empty. Its form is empty. Yet it is full of rain, sunshine, the gardener, and everything that brought it into being."

This sounds terribly deep and important, much like the slogans found on the red banners swaying in the trees nearby. But Thich Nhat Hanh wasn't satisfied with speaking this teaching only; he wanted you to experience it. He had everyone spread their food out in front of them and asked them to contemplate it carefully. "Display what you have for lunch," he said. "Look for the earth, the sky, the sun, the clouds, the rain, the sea in every piece of bread before you put it in your mouth."

When you're hungry, it could be easy to label such remarks as "too profound for me" and simply chow down. But if you do slow yourself and ponder your food carefully for a minute, as Thich Nhat Hanh suggested, you might in fact begin to notice a change in your perception. No longer is your food simply "lunch" to be consumed and forgotten, but rather is composed of separate pieces, each of which is part of an endlessly intricate process that stretches as far back as you'd care to think about it: last season's wheat being grown, harvested, turned to flour and finally a few days ago into bread; decades ago a farmer planting orderly orange groves, which produced the fruit that was squeezed to fill your bottle of juice; the earth-old cycle of evaporation and precipitation that produced the rain that nourished the field that brought forth your carrot sticks. By focusing on *just this*—your everyday lunch spread out before you—you see much more than you did before, your mind has calmed, and your soul has found a place of expansiveness. Thich Nhat Hanh's words are no longer words to believe but rather an experience you've had.

Besides that, it was fun. Approaching lunch in such a way encouraged eating slowly, which allowed you to taste and enjoy your food more fully. "While you eat, if you feel relaxed and joyful," Thich Nhat Hanh added, "that is what the Buddha wanted."

Thich Nhat Hanh had a clipped but gentle and peculiarly comforting way of saying the word "Buddha," such that you could somehow easily substitute in its place "Christ," or "God," or "the universe," or whatever term from your own religious vocabulary that seemed right to you—and yet his words would lose none of their effectiveness. To the critical mind, the words "While you eat, if you feel relaxed and joyful, that is what Jesus wanted" may sound unorthodox and vaguely suspicious, yet this was the gift of Thich Nhat Hanh: to help you recapture the wonder and power of your own faith by sharing with you the experience of his own.

Such was the interfaith spirit of Thich Nhat Hanh's dharma talk, which he gave after lunch. This wasn't a sermon, designed to inspire, scold, or convert, nor was it a lecture designed merely to educate. It was simpler, more direct than that. "People want to end their suffering, but they don't know how," he said with a kind of easygoing certainty, as though he were describing something everybody knew already, as though it were the most obvious thing in the world.

Just then, the sing-songy chimes of an ice cream truck floated through the park and interrupted the dharma talk. The audience shifted uneasily, embarrassed. Thich Nhat Hanh paused briefly, said, "Nice music!" and continued with his talk. The crowd laughed. For everyone else, the ice cream truck was an interruption and a distraction; it was noise. For Thich Nhat Hanh, it was music, just music, and sweet music at that. He had manifested *just this* right there and then, eliminating a form of mild suffering by transforming an uncomfortable moment filled with tension and embarrassment into one of ease and laughter.

Ease and laughter seem to be common states of being for those who spend time around Thich Nhat Hanh, who is a gentle, warm speaker with a gift for articulating what so many of us across the spectrum of faith seem to comprehend on some intuitive level, but never quite express. One woman named Yvonne observed, "I think what Thay says is very wise because it's things we already know. When he says it, we 'remember' it, and it can be very profound."

Thich Nhat Hanh embodies the paradox of being a teacher and leader by not really trying to be one. He called himself a relatively "lazy monk" and observed self-deprecatingly that "Many of us teachers can talk about 'non-Self' for hours and hours, and our Self is very big!" There was something terrific about a teacher who didn't take himself so seriously and who could be both playful and intense. Thich Nhat Hanh's ability to celebrate the vitality of each moment and see in every spiritual path the common theme of people seeking to end their suffering sets him apart. "We need teachers in Buddhism, Christianity, Judaism, and Islam," he said, to help us let go our preoccupations with money, power, fame, and sex. Only then will we move beyond the teachings to experience "true happiness" because then, as Thich Nhat Hanh put it, "the Kingdom of God will be alive!"

And not just alive, but yours—for if you had tasted the expansive power of *just this* for yourself in the park that morning, suddenly, even ordinary things might have seemed more present, more open to you—as if you were moving through the same familiar world that was also, somehow, now a brand-new one. Indeed, walking back to your car along a path near the trees, you might have paused, keys in hand, looking first at the trees, the branches, and the inviting red banners, and then, slowly, at everything else around you—wondering: Could such invitations to expansiveness also be written in the grass, the sky, *everywhere?*

"Come"

*The Greater Los Angeles
Billy Graham Crusade,
November 18–21, 2004
Los Angeles, California*

Most often, going on pilgrimage means just that, "going"—journeying forth from home to find your religious experience, receive your healing, or discover your sought-for spiritual insight. Inherent in the journey is the assumption that what you need, you can't get at home. Although God may be present everywhere, the catalyst to spiritual awakening is found elsewhere, sometimes in a far-off land at the end of a challenging journey.

Sometimes, however, it works the other way around—your catalyst for spiritual awakening or change journeys forth to find *you*, right where you are, just as you are. Though you might find that attending such a traveling pilgrimage that has stopped by your town is less strenuous and requires less sacrifice than, say, making a journey to Medjugorje, these local moments of invitation to encounter the holy right where you stand are no less potent. Indeed, for the very reason that you are near home makes it all the more potent: You're asked to experience God right where you live your everyday life—and that might change things for you. You don't have to journey elsewhere to find God, which is comforting, but you can't leave God behind, either.

One such traveling pilgrimage is the Billy Graham Crusade, a religious and cultural movement of such magnitude and force for personal spiritual renewal that it has become nothing less than an American institution. Indeed, to call Billy Graham an itinerant preacher might be accurate, strictly speaking, but hardly does justice to the scale of a particular Crusade or the cumulative impact Billy Graham has had on the spiritual landscape of America—or, for that matter, the world.

In fact, for those of us raised on color-TV images of whole stadiums listening in rapt attention to this man preaching with might and fervor, it might be hard to imagine that Billy Graham wasn't simply *born* preaching the gospel to an audience of sixty thousand. But what has become a bona fide phenomenon had humble, if auspicious, beginnings.

In September 1949, a young, unknown preacher from North Carolina set up a large tent at the corner of

Washington Boulevard and Hill Street in downtown Los Angeles. Night after night starting at 7:30, and twice on Sundays, he would stand beneath a banner proclaiming "My Life for Christ" and present a simple gospel message. "Every person who rejects Christ and His atoning work is cast into the lake of fire and brimstone," he would begin. "But thanks be to God, He's provided a way out of hell. He's provided a way to heaven . . . because He loves you. . . . God wants you to be saved by accepting and trusting and receiving the Lord Jesus Christ as Savior." It was a straightforward message, to be sure, and this young preacher named Billy Graham didn't pull any punches. Every night he concluded the meeting with an altar call, an invitation for those listening to come forward and make a commitment to Christ: "If you're ever going to be sure you're saved, you'd better do it today. This may be the last chance you will ever have. *Come.*"

Graham had journeyed to Los Angeles with a tent and a Bible, and he put them both to use; before it was all over, some 350,000 people had turned out to hear what this powerful preacher had to say. The success of that one Crusade was pivotal; by inspiring newspaper headlines such as "A New Evangelist Arises," it thrust Billy Graham squarely into America's public eye and set the trajectory for a ministry that would eventually see him travel to more than

185 countries and territories and preach to more people in live audiences than any other man in history.

Fifty-five years to the day that the 1949 L.A. Crusade closed down its tent, Billy Graham, now well into his 80s, was back in Los Angeles for what was widely presumed to be one of his final Crusades. This time, things were different. The Crusade was four days long instead of two months, and instead of preaching to hundreds at a time in a tent on a downtown street corner, he spoke to capacity crowds at the Rose Bowl in Pasadena. But one thing certainly had not changed: Dr. Graham had come with his Bible, and he put it to use.

The 2004 Greater Los Angeles Billy Graham Crusade itself took place over three chilly nights and one clear, brisk Sunday afternoon; a light dusting of snow lay on the San Gabriel Mountains close by to the north. If you had never been to such an event before and you showed up one evening, at first you might have wondered if you had strayed into the wrong event entirely. Every evening as the seats and bleachers filled up, a festival atmosphere prevailed. People ate hot dogs and nachos. One section of the stadium tried to out-cheer another. The spectators started and sustained "the wave" for several circuits around the stadium. It felt like a concert, a sports event—almost anything but a church service. Though there were signs that this was a religious event, it hardly *felt* like that before the evening was over, you were going to be invited to encounter *God* right here in the Rose Bowl.

Yet central to this we'll-come-to-you type of pilgrimage is the conviction that God can—indeed wants—to meet you right where you are. Other kinds of pilgrimages may involve a period of preparation where you slowly and deliberately transition from your everyday mode of being into a place of heightened spiritual awareness in anticipation of a spiritual experience; not so with this kind of pilgrimage. Here, God is entirely able to show up and transform your heart from where it is at this very moment—whether happy or sad, playful or burdened—no questions asked. Your portion of the pilgrimage is comparatively short: Simply answer God's call. God shows up in the here-and-now; in the here-and-now you are asked to respond.

Also central to this kind of pilgrimage is the understanding that you do not have to be in a special, sanctified space in order to encounter God. Many pilgrimage sites are just that—specific *sites* identified as particular, one-of-a-kind centers of spiritual power to which you must travel; not so with this kind of pilgrimage. Here, you can find God anywhere, or more accurately, God's power can transform any place into a hallowed space; hence the Rose Bowl, which is home to the UCLA Bruins football program, became a temporary holy site. The field that weekend bore the telltale grid of white lines and hash marks; yet periodically throughout the Crusade, various speakers referred to how for these four days, at least, the Rose Bowl was no longer a sports arena but through prayer had become a special repository of divine presence and power. "We've made this stadium 'God's house' this week!" exclaimed one speaker.

The speakers may have been speaking metaphorically, but others took the metaphor much more literally. One woman elaborated how she and a dedicated team of other volunteers went through the stands, touching and praying over every single seat, intending that those occupying it during the Crusade would be blessed—an example of the profound belief that God can reach out and touch you *anywhere.*

Another thing that might have surprised you about the Crusade was its thoroughly contemporary flavor. Every night the Crusade opened with a polished multimedia presentation that was followed by two or three popular musical acts such as Michael W. Smith, Third Day, TAIT, and Jars of Clay. Production values were high, complete with light show and effects. Clearly, the Crusade was image-conscious and savvy, intending to appeal to a younger generation than those of us who grew up watching George Beverly Shea singing "Just As I Am" on television. (Shea, now retired from singing for Billy Graham, did give a cameo performance one evening.) One mother said she brought her son and his friend to hear the music; she called it "a rock concert," and she wasn't far off. On some nights, depending on the music, a sort of kinder, gentler, Christian mosh pit coalesced in front of the stage.

Yet the contemporary feel of the show didn't detract from the sense of significance and historical import of this, one of Billy Graham's final Crusade engagements. One college-age man named Bryan found the music and presentation relevant and enjoyable, but he also emphasized the importance of continuity with the past. "We want to be a part of what the movement of God has been in the previous generation. It's said a lot that people my age want something cutting-edge and totally new, and that may be true, but there's something to be said about adding onto a legacy that's already been started. There may be someone here tonight who could be the next Billy Graham. There's something to be said for the torch being passed on."

This sense of history and tradition is important to many pilgrims. They want to feel that they are connecting via the pilgrimage path with those who have gone before them; that they are not spiritual mavericks but rather members of a community of holy and spiritual seekers dedicated to experiencing God in a unique and direct way.

At no time was this sense of historical significance and spiritual import more evident than when, after the music

and preliminary speakers had finished, Billy Graham himself took the stage. As his son assisted him to the podium,
a reverence came over the stadium. Whispers broke out
here and there: "There he is. That's him." When he
reached the pulpit, he took to it with an air of comfortable
authority, as if it were a second home. His hair was
vibrant white, set off all the more against the dark, heavy
overcoat he wore against the cold. He scanned the crowd
silently for a moment. The hush continued—what would
this living legend say? What profound words of wisdom
would he speak? Finally, Graham leaned to the micro-
phone, and his easygoing North Carolina accent rolled
across the stadium. "Well," he said, "I'm glad it's so *warm*
here in Southern California this evening." Spontaneous,
sustained applause broke out and wouldn't let up. It
turned into a standing ovation.

The collective admiration for this man, who was nothing
short of a living legend, was contagious. But when at length
the applause died down and he began to speak in earnest, it
was in the voice of an aging man. Now and again he seemed
to lose his train of thought. Some of his down-home, folksy
illustrations were endearing but dated. Yet time and again
he demonstrated a sharp wit and a concern for contemporary social issues such as racial division, corporate fraud,
and the destruction caused by war. And he always returned

with passion to his fundamental message—salvation through Christ alone.

Indeed, although the music, technology, and scope had changed from his first revival in Los Angeles in 1949, one thing decidedly had not changed: Billy Graham preached his trademark simple, straightforward gospel message. The language was toned down somewhat; gone were references to fire and brimstone, but his message was as clear as ever. "The cross tells us that we are sinners," he proclaimed.

Strong language, yet not offensive, for Graham, whether by natural ability, long years of honing his message, or both, had that peculiar knack for delivering bad news point-blank without coming across as abrupt or insulting. Perhaps this is because what he believed about your soul, he also believed about his own: "The simple fact is that mankind has an evil heart, *all of us*," he emphasized. What Billy Graham preached, Billy Graham understood to be true of everyone, including himself. By not pontificating or making himself into some kind of exception—and you might think, "If anyone is an exception to the 'evil heart' thing, it would probably be Billy Graham"— you felt like he was there with you, down in the trenches of everyday life, helping to show you the way that he himself had discovered to peace of mind and peace with God.

This inclusiveness was remarkably compelling, and his manner of speaking refreshing. In a culture accustomed to excess (including religious excess), cynicism, and political doublespeak, Graham's words were simple, clear, and straightforward. No doubt about it, he was out to convince you of his way of seeing things, but there was no guile. All his motivations were stated; all his cards were on the table. You just got the feeling that there was no ego driving his words.

For most of us, our egos easily give rise to manipulative speech, self-serving behavior, and general small-mindedness. Stripping ourselves of such things is one goal, or at least a frequent result of pilgrimage: By connecting with the holy, with God, with the Source of all good things, we loosen our grip on our self-importance and remember that ultimately we are part of something much larger than ourselves. Billy Graham was so in tune with this that his very speech seemed transparent; his words carried weight, authority, a presence that seemed to come not so much from him as through him.

Many people in attendance described the power they felt working through Billy Graham, a power that paradoxically was inversely proportional to Graham's own strength. "He has aged," said one man who attended all four days of the Crusade, "but the Holy Spirit hasn't. And it's the Holy Spirit in him that you see and hear."

Others, however, recognize the power of Graham's own personality itself. One woman said, "When you think about some of the TV evangelists on cable, you wonder how genuine that is. But when I come here and see Billy Graham, I see calmness and wisdom. It's the feeling of spirit in the venue."

That spirit of calm and wisdom prevailed even in the face of a direct challenge. On one of the nights, Graham was interrupted by a heckler shouting disparagingly at him. Though the man was not visible and his specific words were hard to distinguish, his voice could be plainly heard throughout the stadium. He was even more plainly heard when Billy Graham stopped speaking and stood by patiently. It was an awkward half minute. People looked around at each other: Does Billy Graham know he's being heckled? Or did he lose his place again? He's old—does he even hear that guy?

After a time, the heckling stopped. (Presumably, Rose Bowl security had invited the man to leave.) Then, with a remarkable and radical acceptance of the situation just as it was, Graham said, "That exact thing happened to us here many years ago. God was at work, but we didn't know it then. So I thank God for what's happening now because it's all in his plan."

There, played out before your very eyes, was Billy Graham's profound understanding both that God is active in the here and now, however the situation might look to human eyes, and that God's Spirit, which is marked by patience, acceptance, and trust, can guide our responses to any challenge—a silent (literally) but eloquent testimony that connection with God is possible not just on a wide-ranging pilgrim journey, but at home, every day, every moment.

Billy Graham's actual talk was surprisingly short. "The cross guarantees a future life, in heaven," he said. "The cross says, 'God loves you' and 'God will forgive you.'" As always, he brought the message home with a personal challenge: "But what about you? You go to church, you are a good person. But you're not sure. . . 'Am I saved?'"

Once again, Billy Graham's words had a way of penetrating your outer defenses and gently surrounding your heart, as if the words he was speaking were echoing the questions and doubts you'd long been harboring but had let languish. You felt that his words were spoken out of genuine concern and love for everyone gathered there that night, including *you*.

If there was any doubt, the deep resonance his message found with his audience became apparent enough at the end of the talk. Just as he did in 1949, Billy Graham concluded his preaching with an altar call. He built to it slowly, warning the audience, "In a minute, I'm going to ask you to get up out of your seats and come forward." He explained the reason for his method: "People ask me, 'Why do you ask for a public declaration of faith?' Because in Scripture, every time Christ called someone to follow him, he did it publicly." He returned to the logistics: "From the upper stands it will take you a few minutes, but that's okay. We'll wait for you."

And then with a surprising gentleness, he said simply, "*Come.*"

However you might understand it or whatever you might call it—Billy Graham's own personality, the power of God, or the force of transformation in the world—it was pulsing in that word, "Come." Spoken by Billy Graham, it was a word of astonishing power.

"Bring your families, bring your friends," he continued. "Come. We have counselors here for you. If you don't speak English, we have counselors who speak your language. You get up and come."

People hardly needed additional encouragement. Even before he issued the invitation, some people began to stir and made their way to the aisles so they could be among the first to be down on the field. And once Graham said, "Come," a gentle mass movement began. People left their seats and headed for the aisle. Whole rows emptied. The steps became rivers of pilgrims flowing down to the field, unhurried but urgent, as if they expected to find their destiny there.

Watching the dozens, then hundreds, then thousands of people make their way solemnly down the steps—a kind of mini-pilgrimage, from seat to field—you might have wondered about the frivolity that reigned throughout the stadium earlier in the evening. How could so many people make such a rapid transition from festive to serious after a few words from an old preacher culminating in the single-word invitation "Come"? Yet appearances are deceptive; though this pilgrimage walk looks brief and easy, the journey for those responding began long ago. Who is to say when God first planted the desire for spiritual transformation in a person's life? Who can know how that need was nurtured over weeks or months or years? Is there any way to adequately understand how that word spoken by Billy Graham, "Come," itself became the final catalyst for spiritual transformation in that moment, in that place?

As the people streamed down, the choir sang "Just As I Am," underscoring the understanding that God is accessible in the here and now, whatever the circumstances. Billy Graham himself leaned on the pulpit, watching the field fill with people responding to his call. His mouth was closed as he watched; he looked like a stern, tired, but patient father. But when he spoke again, his words were soothing and welcoming. "If you don't remember a thing I've said tonight, I hope you remember God loves you." After another minute, he'd say, "There may not be another tomorrow for you. Don't you let anyone stop you from coming." In another minute, he'd repeat it again, "Come."

At length the field filled with people, from the stage at the twenty-yard line all the way across midfield to the opposite twenty-yard line, with people spilling out-of-bounds. Billy Graham prayed a short prayer; those on the field repeated the prayer after him, inviting Christ into their lives, either for the first time or as what he called a rededication. Each night, at the conclusion of the prayer, sustained applause broke out. The emcee explained it to those gathered on the field: "People are applauding because they're welcoming you into the family of faith."

From Los Angeles in 1949 to Los Angeles in 2004, Billy Graham had come full circle. The scope and approach of his Crusade had changed, but the man and his message had not. His final crusade there was a tip of the hat for that city's role in launching his ministry, which he summed up in simple fashion on the Crusade's final night, just before he left the pulpit for the final time. "I thank you all for the privilege of being here," he said. "In Jesus' name, Amen."

ACKNOWLEDGMENTS

This project would not have been possible without the support, friendship and encouragement of many people. We wish to thank our patient and thoughtful editor, Lil Copan, who first had the idea for this book and has been a delight to work with; our agent, Linda Roghaar; and also the creative and hardworking people at Paraclete Press, including Carol Showalter, Jennifer Lynch, Lillian Miao, Sister Mercy, Pamela Jordan, and Jon Sweeney.

Jana would like to acknowledge Kelly Hughes, who was a huge help when Jana was researching the Graceland and Saint Jude chapters, even navigating Chicago traffic and locating the best taco joint. She got only an Elvis keychain for all her efforts. As always, Kelly's friendship and enthusiasm make any work a pleasure. Phyllis and Sam Tickle provided a place to stay at The Farm in Lucy on a trip to Tennessee, with warm laughter and Memphis barbecue all around. Jana wishes to thank Gray Henry, who knows everyone on the planet and wants to get them all to be friends, for first picking up the phone and getting everything started with Gethsemani. She'd also like to acknowledge many of the people who gave their time and stories to be interviewed for these chapters: Dianne Aprile, Brother

Frederic, Brother Raphael, Father Anton, John French, Mary French, John Ingwersen, Dave Krueger, Betty Mitman, Steve Pollick, Judy Roberts, Sister Agnes, Sister Gabriella, Sister Helen, Sister Teresa, and Blair Tingley. Tom Bremer shared his extensive knowledge of religious tourism and pointed to valuable source materials, and Timothy Beal offered helpful encouragement on the Graceland chapter.

Mark wishes to acknowledge and thank Melvin Fujikawa for his help and suggestions; Rick and Lori Taylor for enthusiastically sharing the Healing Rooms experience; Brother Will Brown and Brother Lawrence Harms for sitting in the splendid library one afternoon and generously sharing about life at Mt. Calvary; Denise Cruz for true and astonishing tales of dangerous travel in foreign lands; to the many brave people who were willing to be interviewed by a tape-recorder-wielding total stranger; and especially Jana Riess, for inviting me to be a part of this project in the first place.

NOTES

INTRODUCTION

p. xviii . . . *other languages have distinctive terms for different forms of pilgrimage,* David Souden, *Pilgrimage: Twenty Journeys to Inspire the Soul.* (Wheaton, IL: Quest Books/The Ivy Press, 2001), 49. Souden's full-color coffee-table book includes twenty very different kinds of pilgrimage experiences, from Marian apparition sites and Catholic shrines to Native American holy places; the Muslim *hajj*; Buddhist, Mormon, and Sikh temples; and places like Lourdes that are renowned for their healing properties.

p. xviii . . . *But the truth is that every pilgrimage is unique.* One of the best general introductions to pilgrimage is Phil Cousineau's excellent *The Art of Pilgrimage: The Seeker's Guide to Making Travel Sacred* (Berkeley, CA: Conari, 1998). Cousineau draws from his own experiences and the lives of other pilgrims, and discusses visits to sites all over the world. He also helpfully unpacks the experience of pilgrimage step-by-step, from the longing and the call to the departure, journey, arrival, and return.

p. xxi *How might we use that wisdom to see more soulfully . . . ?* Cousineau, *The Art of Pilgrimage*, xxvii.

PART I

Pilgrimages of Healing

INTRODUCTION

p. 3 "... *when the water was 'stirred up' and its powers activated.*" John 5:2-3, 7.

p. 3 "... *whatever disease that person had.*" John 5:4.

p. 5 "... *patron saint of seemingly impossible or desperate causes.*" www.stjudeleague.org.

ONE

The Lourdes of America
El Santuario de Chimayó

p. 7 *hundreds of thousands of pilgrims who journey here every year.* Archdiocese of Santa Fe, "El Santuario de Chimayó, the Lourdes of America," http://www.archdiocesesantafe.org/AboutASF/Chimayo.html.

p. 12 *in the location where he was discovered.* Sons of the Holy Family, *El Santuario . . . A Stop on the "High Road to Taos"* (Silver Spring, MD: Sons of the Holy Family, 1994), 10.

p. 13 *Don Bernardo built a chapel on the spot.* Stephen F. de Borhegyi, "The Miraculous Shrines of Our Lord of Esquípulas in Guatemala and Chimayó, New Mexico," in *El Santuario de Chimayó*, ed. by The Spanish Colonial Arts Society, Inc. (Santa Fe: Ancient City Press, 1956), 18.

p. 13 *. . . it in order to take advantage of its healing powers.* Elizabeth Kay, *Chimayó Valley Traditions* (Santa Fe: Ancient City Press, 1987), 5–17.

TWO

Finding Jude the Obscure
The National Shrine of Saint Jude

p. 22 *Tradition holds that he was married and had at least one child*, Liz Trotta, *Jude: A Pilgrimage to the Saint of Last Resort* (HarperSanFrancisco, 1998) 118 and 129.

p. 22 *This sketch is not much on which to base a successful and highly specialized devotional cult.* The use of the word "cult" in Roman Catholicism is not pejorative; it connotes devotion to a particular saint or religious figure. This usage does not in any way imply that devotees are brainwashed or misguided.

p. 23 *his veneration didn't get off the ground in a major way until the 1920s.* For an excellent history of the devotion to Jude in the United States, see Robert Orsi, *Thank You, Saint Jude!: Women's Devotion to the Patron Saint of Hopeless Causes* (New Haven: Yale University, 1996).

p. 23 *the closing of local steel mills in February of 1929 had put many parishioners out of work.* See the video "Turn to Saint Jude, a Faithful Friend," hosted by Will Shaw.

p. 23 *The local priest, Father Tort, estimated that ninety percent of the families in the parish had no regular paycheck.* See http://www.stjudeleague.org/history.htm for a brief history of the Shrine.

p. 24 *this sudden outpouring of affection marked him as an overnight sensation.* Orsi, *Thank You, Saint Jude!*, 22.

p. 27 *Pray for me, I am so helpless and alone.* There are several slight variations of the Jude prayer; this rendition is from a card purchased at the National Shrine.

p. 28 *Consider the case of Henry Green.* Henry Green and Judith both recount their stories in the video "Turn to Saint Jude, a Faithful Friend." Since they chose to use their real names there, we have followed that preference here. When we've quoted a person from a website, we use whatever name they called themselves.

p. 31 *"God bless you and thank you for shining your light in my son's life."* Many people have recorded their personal experiences with Jude at www.stjudenovena.org/testimonies/

p. 31 *. . . shrines in Baltimore, San Francisco, Rome and other cities.* For a fascinating look at some of these other Jude shrines, see Liz Trotta, *Jude: A Pilgrimage to the Saint of Last Resort.*

p. 32 *"The impalpability of Jude is the essence of his appeal."* Liz Trotta, *Jude*, 13.

THREE

Love Is in Itself Healing
The Healing Rooms of the Santa Maria Valley

p. 35 *"they will lay hands on the sick, and they will recover."* International Association of Healing Rooms http://www.healingrooms.com/index.php?src=content&cid=1.

p. 35 *France, Holland, Israel, Zambia, Korea, and Singapore* International Association of Healing Rooms, "International Association of Healing Rooms (IAHR) Members," http://www.healingrooms.com/index.php?src=location&l=2.

PART II

Pilgrimages of Benedictine Hospitality

INTRODUCTION

p. 55 *"He will say: 'I was a stranger and you took Me in'"* Matthew 25:35.

p. 55 *"... of the household of the faith"* Galatians 6:10.

FOUR

Safe House

The Community of Jesus

p. 58 *a nosedive in the number of young applicants.* For more on the crisis of vocations within the Roman Catholic Church, see Charles Morris, *American Catholic: The Story of the People, Passion, and Politics Behind America's Largest and Most Influential Church* (New York: Times Books, 1997) and Donald Cozzens, *Sacred Silence: Denial and the Crisis in the Church* (Collegeville, MN: Liturgical Press, 2002).

p. 59 *Community members are expected to speak the truth to one another in love.* The author of Ephesians writes, "But speaking the truth in love, we must grow up in every way unto him who is the head, into Christ, from whom the whole body, joined and knit together by every ligament with which it is equipped, as each part is working properly, promotes the body's growth in building itself up in love" Ephesians 4:15-16.

p. 69 *"Elisha feeding the one hundred"* 2 Kings 4:42–44.

p. 69 *"the indebted widow whose vessels were inexplicably filled with oil 2"* Kings 4:1–7.

FIVE

Psalms and Silence
The Abbey of Gethsemani

p. 76 *"the products of our factories and printing presses and movie studios and all the rest."* Thomas Merton, *The Seven Storey Mountain* (New York: Harcourt Brace Jovanovich, 1948), 133.

p. 77 *without having to carry on a conversation with a single stranger.* In his chapter "'Silence Is Spoken Here': Trappists and Trappistines," novelist Brad Gooch recounts an entertaining story about that anonymity. Apparently, during the week that Gooch made a retreat at the monastery, film actor Ethan Hawke was also there, and his presence attracted some whispers not only among the retreatants but among some of the monks as well. See *Godtalk: Travels in Spiritual America* (New York: Knopf, 2002), 172. However, this experience is far from typical.

p. 81 *he was the first American Trappist monk to receive permission to live alone. Merton: A Film Biography*, produced by Paul Wilkes and Audrey L. Glynn (First Run Features, 1984).

p. 82 *flagellated themselves over the shoulders for any infractions of the Rule.* Dianne Aprile, *The Abbey of Gethsemani*, 80.

p. 82 . . . *decided to begin receiving women pilgrims.* Dianne Aprile, *Making a Heart for God: A Week Inside a Catholic Monastery* (Woodstock, VT: SkyLight Paths, 2000), 20-21.

p. 84 *personal and monastic crises, and innumerable natural disasters.* Aprile, *The Abbey of Gethsemani*, 133.

SEVEN

St. Peregrine, Pray for Us
Mission San Juan Capistrano

p. 111 *intercede on behalf of cancer sufferers in particular.* "Saint Peregrine Shrine for Cancer Sufferers" (pamphlet distributed at Mission San Juan Capistrano, 2004).

p. 115 *a journey of some 7,500 miles.* Mission San Juan Capistrano, "History," http://www.missionsjc.com/swallows.html

p. 119 *A statue of St. John of Capistrano . . . stands near the front.* "Mission Guide: San Juan Capistrano" (pamphlet distributed at Mission San Juan Capistrano, 2004).

EIGHT

The Mountains are Singing
Beauty and Devotion among the Red Rocks

p. 126 *in what by then had become a desert land.* Wayne Ranney, *Sedona through Time: Geology of the Red Rocks* (Flagstaff, AZ: Zia Interpretive Services, 2001), 13–24; 66–72.

p. 128 *two-thirds are seeking a spiritual experience.* "Vortex Sites Are Popular," *Recreation Guide to Your National Forest: Red Rock Country—Coconino National Forest—Sedona, Arizona* (Sedona, AZ: United States Department of Agriculture—Forest Service), 11.

p. 131 *nodes of spiritual energy that became popularized in the 1980s.* Dennis Andres, *What Is a Vortex?* (Sedona, AZ: Meta Adventures, 2000), 28.

p. 131 *"whether on a physical, mental, emotional, or spiritual level."* Andres, 12-13.

p. 133 *". . . monument to cooperation and religious beliefs."*
City of Sedona, "Arts and Religion,"
http://www.sedonaaz.gov/sedona/history15.aspx.

p. 137 *"so charged with God, that it spurs man's spirit godward!"*
Marguerite Brunswig Staude, "Chapel of the Holy Cross"
(pamphlet distributed at the Chapel of the Holy Cross, 2004).

NINE

Finding Grace in the Land
Elvis Presley as a Secular Saint

p. 148 *. . . draws some 600,000 visitors annually.* For statistics on
visitors to Graceland, see Amy Wilson, "If the King Is Dead, It's
Been 28 Years." *Lexington Herald-Leader* (August 14, 2005),
E-2.

p. 150 *Elvis bought it in 1957 for just over $100,000.* Peter
Guralnick, *Last Train to Memphis: The Rise of Elvis Presley.*
(Boston: Little, Brown, and Company, 1994), 397.

p. 155 *we are reminded that Elvis has a hunka burnin' love for
whosoever believeth in him.* http://www.geocities.com/presley-
terian_church/home.html.

p. 157 *. . . testifies to the strength of a religion in the making.* After
Jana had drafted this chapter, Tom Bremer pointed her toward
Erika Doss's fascinating book *Elvis Culture: Fans, Faith, and
Image* (University of Kansas Press, 1999). Doss's chapter on
"Saint Elvis" and her photographs of the artwork and shrines
that fans have created were very helpful. Also, Tom's own book
Blessed with Tourists: The Borderlands of Religion and Tourism

in San Antonio (University of North Carolina, 2004) has been helpful in conceptualizing the difference between pilgrimage and tourism, not just for Graceland but for all the chapters in this book.

p. 160 *she spent much of her adolescence under Elvis's roof.* Bobbie Ann Mason, *Elvis Presley: A Penguin Life* (New York: Lipper/Viking, 2003), 90, 98–100.

p. 161 *"We identify with her because we could see our tears in her eyes."* Forrest Church's thoughts on Princess Diana and Mother Teresa are from *Lifecraft: The Art of Meaning in the Everyday* (Boston: Beacon Press, 2000), 44.

The Greater Los Angeles Billy Graham Crusade,
November 18–21, 2004

p. 178 *"This may be the last chance you will ever have. Come."* Billy Graham, "The Road to Hell—and the Way of Salvation: A Message by Billy Graham," *decision*, November 2004, 2–5.

p. 179 . . . *to more people in live audiences than any other man in history.* Billy Graham Evangelistic Association, "Bios: William (Billy) F. Graham," http://www.billygraham.org/mediaRelations/bios.asp?p=1.

Getting There
Resources for Further Information

EL SANTUARIO DE CHIMAYÓ

For an excellent account of the history and traditions surrounding El Santuario de Chimayó, see *Chimayo Valley Traditions* (Ancient City Press, 1987) by Elizabeth Kay. A helpful website is maintained by the Archdiocese of Santa Fe at http://www.archdiocesesantafe.org/AboutASF/Chimayó.html, which includes visiting hours and a schedule of Masses held at El Santuario.

THE NATIONAL SHRINE OF SAINT JUDE

For an examination of St. Jude's recent rise from obscurity, see journalist Liz Trotta's *Jude: A Pilgrimage to the Saint of Last Resort* (HarperSanFrancisco, 1998). For a study of the National Shrine of St. Jude in Chicago specifically, see *Thank You, St. Jude: Women's Devotion to the Patron Saint of Hopeless Causes* (Yale University Press, 1996), by Robert Orsi. For history, current happenings, "prayer opportunities," a virtual gift shop, and directions to the National Shrine of St. Jude, visit http://shrineofsaintjude.com.

HEALING ROOMS OF THE SANTA MARIA VALLEY

For more testimonies of healing, hours of operation, and directions to the Healing Rooms of the Santa Maria Valley, go to http://www.healingroomssmv.com. For information about the International Association of Healing Rooms, which includes a listing of all member Healing Rooms near you and across the world, visit www.healingrooms.com/index.php.

THE COMMUNITY OF JESUS

For a take-home experience of the Community of Jesus, check out *The Little Book of Hours: Praying with the Community of Jesus* (Paraclete Press, 2004), which adapts the Community's daily Liturgy of the Hours as a model for personal or communal worship. Visit www.communityofjesus.org for information about the Community, including the new Church of the Transfiguration, the role of the arts in community life, a schedule of events, and more.

THE ABBEY OF GETHSEMANI

Explore the legacy of the Abbey of Gethsemani at www.monks.org. *The Abbey of Gethsemani: Place of Peace and Paradox* (Trout Lily Press, 1998) and *Making a Heart for God: A Week Inside a Catholic Monastery* (SkyLight

Paths, 2000) both by Dianne Aprile, give an insider's view of life in the monastery.

MT. CALVARY RETREAT HOUSE AND MONASTERY

Find information on the Order of the Holy Cross and retreats at Mt. Calvary, along with the beautiful calligraphy created by one of the brothers, at www.mount-calvary.org. For detailed information on staying at Mt. Calvary and dozens of other monastic retreat houses, see *Sanctuaries: The Complete United States—A Guide to Lodgings in Monasteries, Abbeys, and Retreats* (Bell Tower, 1996), by Jack and Marcia Kelly.

MISSION SAN JUAN CAPISTRANO

For a detailed history of Mission San Juan Capistrano, visit www.missionsjc.com or read *San Juan Capistrano* (Arcadia Publishing, 2005) by Pamela Hallan-Gibson, Don Tryon, Mary Ellen Tryon, and the San Juan Capistrano Historical Society. For an accessible general history of the California mission system, see *The California Missions* (Sunset Publishing, 1979) by Sunset Editors.

SEDONA, ARIZONA

For a user-friendly and inspiring explanation of the vortex phenomena in Sedona, read *What is a Vortex?: Sedona's Vortex Sites—a Practical Guide* (Meta Adventures, 2000) by Dennis Andres. A spirited primer on the geology of the area is *Sedona through Time: Geology of the Red Rocks* (Zia Interpretive Services, 2001) by Wayne Ranney. To just get out and hike, take along *Sedona Hikes: 130 Day Hikes and 5 Vortex Sites around Sedona, Arizona,* revised eighth ed. (Hexagon Press, 2004) by Richard K. Mangum. The City of Sedona maintains an informative and useful website at www.sedonaaz.gov.

ELVIS

Elvis lives! at www.elvis.com, which includes information on the man, the music, and the mansion—even an opportunity to "explore your inner Elvis." Join the faithful at The First Presleyterian Church of Elvis the Divine at www.geocities.com/presleyterian_church. For another look at Elvis's life and legacy, see *Careless Love: The Unmaking of Elvis Presley* (Little, Brown, 1999) by Peter Guralnick, or *Elvis Presley: The Man. The Life. The Legend.* (Atria, 2004) by Pamela Clarke Keogh.

Thich Nhat Hanh

Among the most popular of Thich Nhat Hanh's many books are *Living Buddha, Living Christ* (Riverhead Books, 1995) and *The Miracle of Mindfulness* (Beacon Press, 1999). Plum Village's website is www.plumvillage.org, which contains Thich Nhat Hanh's travel schedule and links to dharma centers in the United States affiliated with Plum Village and Thich Nhat Hanh.

Billy Graham

Billy Graham's own reflections on his life and ministry are recorded in his autobiography, *Just As I Am* (HarperSanFrancisco, 1997). For the continuing work of the Billy Graham Evangelistic Association, see www.billy-graham.org.

About Paraclete Press

Who We Are

Paraclete Press is an ecumenical publisher of books and recordings on Christian spirituality. Our publishing represents a full expression of Christian belief and practice—from Catholic to Evanglical, from Protestant to Orthodox.

Paraclete Press is the publishing arm of the Community of Jesus, an ecumenical monastic community in the Benedictine tradition. As such, we are uniquely positioned in the marketplace without connection to a large corporation and with informal relationships to many branches and denominations of faith.

We like it best when people buy our books from booksellers, our partners in successfully reaching as wide an audience as possible.

What We Are Doing

Books

Paraclete Press publishes books that show the richness and depth of what it means to be Christian. Although Benedictine spirituality is at the heart of all that we do, we publish books that reflect the Christian experience across many cultures, time periods, and houses of worship.

We publish books that nourish the vibrant life of the church and its people—books about spiritual practice, formation, history, ideas, and customs.

We have several different series of books within Paraclete Press, including the bestselling *Living Library* series of modernized classic texts; *A Voice from the Monastery*—giving voice to men and women monastics about what it means to live a spiritual life today; award winning literary faith fiction; and books that explore Judaism and Islam and discover how these faiths inform Christian thought and practice.

Recordings

From Gregorian chant to contemporary American choral works, our music recordings celebrate the richness of sacred choral music through the centuries. Paraclete is proud to distribute the recordings of the internationally acclaimed choir Gloriæ Dei Cantores, who have been praised for their "rapt and fathomless spiritual intensity" by *American Record Guide*, and the Gloriæ Dei Cantores Schola, which specializes in the study and performance of Gregorian chant. Paraclete is also the exclusive North American distributor of the Monastic Choir of St. Peter's Abbey in Solesmes, France, long considered to be a leading authority on Gregorian chant performance.

Learn more about us at our website:
www.paracletepress.com, or call us toll-free at
1-800-451-5006.